P9-EJU-869

Every Eye Beholds You

EVERY EYE BEHOLDS YOU

A World Treasury of Prayer

Edited and Annotated by Thomas J. Craughwell

Introduction by Karen Armstrong

QUALITY PAPERBACK BOOK CLUB
NEW YORK

Copyright © 1998 by Thomas J. Craughwell. All rights reserved.

Every Eye Beholds You: A World Treasury of Prayer is a publication of Quality Paperback Book Club, 1271 Avenue of the Americas, New York, New York 10020.

Acknowledgment of permission to reprint copyrighted materials can be found starting on page 317. All best efforts have been made to contact the owners of copyrighted material reprinted here. The editor would be pleased to hear from copyright holders who could not be found so that the proper acknowledgments might be made.

Book design by Irene Lipton
Illustrations by Christopher Russell

Printed in the United States of America

For my mother and father

Prayer is the mother and daughter of tears. It is an expiation of sin, a bridge across temptation, a bulwark against affliction. It wipes out conflict, is the work of angels, and is the nourishment of everything spiritual.

Saint John Climacus, *The Ladder of Divine Ascent*

TABLE OF CONTENTS

Aside from the essential prayers of the major religious traditions that are a necessary part of this collection, I selected prayers that struck me as especially beautiful or affecting.

I made an effort to find prayers in their traditional form. It seems to me there is comfort in repeating ancient prayers: their timeless formulas are a bridge between one who recites the prayer today and all those faithful souls throughout the centuries who prayed in the exact same words.

For prayers taken from the Bible, I used the King James version because it is the most beautiful translation of the Scriptures in English. For prayers taken from the Book of Wisdom, a book that does not appear in the King James Bible, I used the Catholic Douay-Rheims translation, the exact contemporary of the King James and its only rival for beauty of language.

From time to time, readers will encounter inconsistencies in the text. Some transliterated Hebrew prayers begin "Baruch ata," others begin "Baruch atah." Some Muslim prayers address Allah and others address God. In some places Muhammad is the Prophet and in others he is the Messenger. I would have liked everything to be tidy and uniform, but translators and transliterators will differ and I felt obliged to be faithful to my sources.

Writing a book may appear to be a solitary task, but in fact I was helped and supported by many people right from the start. My first word of thanks goes to André Bernard, who suggested that I compile an anthology of prayers.

I was very fortunate to have Les Pockell direct this project. He had wonderful ideas that improved this book immeasurably. And he is a very patient man—an indispensable quality in an editor.

Lisa Thornbloom organized my messy manuscript into a coherent whole, secured permissions from a host of sources, and never let an important detail escape her notice.

I am especially grateful to James O'Halloran, librarian of the Maryknoll Seminary Library in Maryknoll, New York, and Karen Jermyn and Eleana Silk of the Saint Vladimir Seminary Library in Yonkers, New York. They gave me free access to their excellent collections.

My thanks to J. M. Kore Salvato and Sharif Graham, who introduced me to the prayers of the Sufis; Rabbi David K. Holtz and Cantor Margot Bermas of

Temple Beth Abraham in Tarrytown, New York, for their assistance in finding transliterations of Hebrew prayers; and Ubai Nooruddin, who explained to me the essentials of prayer in Islam.

Finally, my thanks to Bill Soleim, Debbie VanderBilt, Colin Soleim, and Candis La Prade. Through them, I found some of the best material in this book.

—Thomas J. Craughwell
March 1998

BY KAREN ARMSTRONG

We tend to equate faith with believing certain things about God or the sacred. A religious person is often called a "believer" and seen as one who has adopted the correct ideas about the divine. Belief is thus seen as the first and essential step of the spiritual journey. Before we embark on a religious life, which must make considerable demands on our moral, social, professional, and personal affairs, we think that we must first satisfy ourselves intellectually that there *is* a God or that the truths of our particular tradition—Jewish, Christian, Muslim, Buddhist, Hindu, or whatever—are valid. It seems pointless to make a commitment unless we are convinced about the essentials. In our modern, scientific world, this makes good, rational sense: First you establish a principle, and then you apply it.

But the history of religion makes it clear that this is not how it works. To expect to have faith before embarking on the disciplines of the spiritual life is like putting the cart before the horse. In all the great traditions, prophets, sages, and mystics spend very little time telling their disciples what they ought to *believe*. Indeed, it is only since the Enlightenment that faith has been defined as intellectual submission to a creed. Hitherto, faith had been seen as a virtue rather than a prerequisite. It meant trust, and was used in rather the same way as when we say that we have faith *in* a person or an ideal. Faith was thus a carefully cultivated conviction that, despite all the tragic and dispiriting evidence to the contrary, our lives did have some ultimate meaning and value. You could not possibly arrive at faith in this sense before you had lived a religious life. Faith was thus the fruit of spirituality, not something that you had to have at the start of your quest.

All the great teachers of spirituality in all the major traditions have, therefore, insisted that before you can have faith, you must live in a certain way. You must lead a compassionate life, transcending the demands of the clamorous ego and recognizing the sacred in others; you must perform rituals (often enshrined in religious law) that make even the most mundane detail of our lives an encounter with the ultimate; all traditions insist that you must also pray. Prayer is thus not born of belief and intellectual conviction; it is a practice that creates faith.

This remarkable anthology shows the universality of prayer. Hindus, Buddhists, Native Americans, African tribespeople, Jews, Christians, and

Muslims all have very different *beliefs*, yet when they address the sacred, they do so in strikingly similar ways. It is surprising that prayer is such a universal practice, since it is fraught with problems. Everybody insists that the ultimate and the transcendent—called variously God, Nirvana, Brahman, or the sacred—cannot be defined in words or concepts, and yet, as these pages show, men and women habitually attempt to speak to the divine. Why do they do this, and what are the implications of this verbal attempt to bridge the yawning gulf that separates us from the sacred? Many Hindus, for example, see Brahman as strictly impersonal: It cannot, therefore, be addressed as "Thou"; it cannot speak to human beings nor relate to them in a personal way; it cannot "love" or get "angry." But at the same time, Brahman sustains and pervades *us*. It is so bound up with our very existence that it is not really appropriate to speak *to* it or think *about* it, as though it were a separate entity. And yet, as this volume shows, Hindus pray like the rest of us. They thank, they beseech, they crave forgiveness. Why?

Prayer, one might think, should be easier for Jews, Christians, and Muslims, since their God is experienced as a personal being. As the Bible and the Koran show, he can get angry and feel love for us; he can speak to us and encounter us. Even so, there are difficulties. Does God really need to be told by us that he created the world and redeemed us and that we are miserable sinners? Surely he knows all this already. Does he demand that we thank him, praise him, and plead for mercy? There is something slightly repellant in this notion, as it suggests a despotic deity who demands endless sycophantic obeisance from his worshipers. And what does it mean to refer, as I have just done, to God as "he"? Theologians constantly remind us that God goes beyond all human categories, including that of gender. Yet it is so difficult to avoid gender words—to say nothing of the limiting and even abhorrent ways in which such qualities as "anger," "love," and the like suggest a God who is all too human. All talk of and to God stumbles under great difficulties. Is there not a danger that our prayers will anthropomorphize God, making "him" loom in our imaginations as a being like ourselves only writ large, with feelings, intentions, and inadequacies similar to our own? If we are not careful, our prayers can cut God down to size and help us to create a deity in our own images and likenesses. Such a God can only be an idol and hence offensive to the true spirit of monotheism.

The prayers in this book show that when men and women pray, they are in some profound sense talking to themselves. This does not mean that they are not also addressing the ultimate, since all the world's faiths do not see the sacred as simply Something "out there" but as a Reality that is also encountered in the depths of our own beings. But it is also true that people who pray are addressing deep personal needs and fears. We live in a frightening world and are the prey of mortality, injustice, cruelty, disaster, darkness, and an evil that can seem palpable and overwhelming. Unlike other animals, we humans fall very easily into despair. The prayers in this volume show that from a very early date, people have made themselves confront their terrors. They have invoked them, described them to themselves in prayer (as well as in art—a related activity), and in so doing have managed to reach beyond them. Men and women have always sensed that there is, in spite of the horrors that flesh is heir to, "an ultimate rightness of things," a Beneficence that is not only outside them but within. Prayers, such as that of Saint Patrick, attempt to invoke that benign power and strength that will enable us finally to lighten the darkness in the depths of the self.

We rarely allow ourselves to voice these deep fears and anxieties. We are all struggling to survive. We cannot afford to admit our weakness and terror too freely. We are fearful of burdening others; we do not want to appear weak or open ourselves to exploitation in the battle that is life. We protect ourselves in all kinds of ways, especially by means of words. We are cautious and defensive and use language to bolster our sense of self for our own sakes as well as to impress others. We are rarely willing to admit our shortcomings and are quick to respond to a slight with a verbal counteroffensive. We make jokes to ward off our sense of life's tragedy or to make others (whom we fear or envy) objects of ridicule. We have fits of meanness in which we feel impaired by others' success. We exalt our own achievements, scuttle over our humiliations, shield ourselves from hurt, and make derogatory remarks about those who threaten our sense of security in ways that we do not always understand. We thus turn our words into weapons that attack as well as defend. All such activity embeds us in the prison of our own frightened egos.

Prayer helps us to liberate ourselves and to use language in an entirely different way, as these pages show. In prayer, we learn to acknowledge our vulnerability, our frailty, our failures, and our sins. By putting our unutterable weaknesses into words, we make them more real to ourselves but also make them more manageable. When we admit that we need forgiveness, we realize in a new way that this will be impossible unless we also forgive. We give voice to our neediness, our longing, our terror. This daily discipline helps us to break through the defensive carapaces that we all form around ourselves, thus allowing the Benevolence and Rightness for which we long to penetrate the prisons of our cautionary being.

This process can be discerned in nearly every section of this book but especially in the prayers of the mystics. These geniuses of spirituality have learned the difficult art of opening themselves to something greater. They speak of the importance of ridding ourselves of negativity and defensiveness; of accepting the realities of suffering and imperfection; and of becoming aware of our longing for Something that transcends the pettiness and anxiety of our self-bound existence. Mystics also praise the virtue of voluntary poverty, which divests the self of the possessiveness that can only impede our progress. They speak of a Wisdom that is not an achievement of our own, to be used to advance our egotism and to help us to exploit the world and others for our own benefit; this wisdom is instead seen as a gift and attribute of the divine.

But prayer is not only an expression of fragility. Human beings have always experienced the world with awe and wonder. Despite the terrors and sorrows of the cosmos, its grandeur and beauty fill us with delight. It seems that the more we learn about the world, the more this sense of wonder increases. We used to think that science would eliminate this and make the mystery of the universe plain. But this has not happened. Sometimes, cosmologists and physicists today appear to be creating a new type of religious discourse, making us confront the dark world of uncreated reality as the mystics did and forcing us to see that the nature of existence exceeds the narrow compass of our minds. Thus, science, which can impart a false sense of pride and self-sufficiency, can also impart a humbling experience of our ignorance, smallness, and limitations. It can lead us to that attitude of silent awe of which the great contemplatives speak.

Yet the sheer busy-ness of our lives often leaves little time for contemplation. The world can become familiar to us. The prayers of praise and thanksgiving in this volume help to correct this. When they list the wonders of creation, these prayers are not grovelling attempts to flatter the Creator but serve to remind us of the marvels that exist all around us. They thus help us to see what is really there: a mystery that cannot be simplistically defined but that becomes apparent when we learn how to strip away the veil of familiarity that obscures it. Such prayers help to hold us in the attitude of wonder that is characteristic of the best religion. Other prayers help us to put ourselves in tune with the fundamental laws of existence, to submit ourselves to the rhythms of the seasons and the cosmos. By cultivating a sense of these great laws and truths, our own egotistical concerns are put into perspective. By learning to see the sacred in the world around us, we will approach it with reverence. The world becomes what Muslims call an *ayah* (a sign) of God, not something to be exploited or greedily ransacked for our gain. Finally, such prayers of thanksgiving help us to cultivate that sense of gratitude that is so often difficult to achieve in our daily battle for survival. When we feel insecure, it is sometimes hard to express the debt we owe to others for our achievements. By making us list the benefits we have received and give voice to our thanks, prayer helps us to acquire a warm, inner sense of favors received. Instead of feeling hard done by, we learn that we are perhaps more fortunate than we know.

Prayers thus create an attitude from which true faith and conviction can grow. But they are never ends in themselves: Most traditions have taught men and women to go beyond words into the Silence beyond through the repetition of a mantra (some of which appear in this book). These teach us that our words cannot define God or the divine mystery, no matter how eloquent our prayer. They can serve only as springboards to the sacred, helping us to open ourselves to the deeper currents of existence and thus to live more intensely and fully.

But prayer cannot be effective unless it is accompanied by the ethical practices of religion, particularly by the virtue of compassion, which, all the major religions insist, is the one and only test of true spirituality. All too often, however, religious people can fall into the trap of self-righteousness and intolerance. Some find it impossible to believe that other traditions are valid paths to the divine. This book should help to correct such a tendency. By learning to pray the prayers of people who do not share our *beliefs*, we can learn at a level deeper than the cerebral to value their *faith*.

PRONUNCIATION GUIDE

Arabic

a as in *hat*
i as in *hit*
u as in *put*
ai as in *aisle*
au as in *auburn*
gh as in *gain*
q/kh as in *cave*

Greek

a as in *father*
e/i/ei/oi/ui as in *feet*
e/ai in *bet*
o as in *own*
ou as in *too*
g as in *get*
gk as in *gutter*
hr as in *Christ*
th as in *thee*
tz as in *adze*
mp as b in *butter*
nt as d in *dental*

Hebrew

a/ah as in *father*
e/eh as in *get*
i as in *big*
o as in *most*
u as in *boot*
ch/h/kh as in the Scottish word *loch*
g/gh when followed by any vowel as in *good*
ph as in *food*

Latin

a as in *father*
e as in *red*
i as in *feet*
o as in *for*
u as in *moon*
ae/oe as in *red*
ui, when preceded by q or ng, as in *we*

In certain cases, when two vowels come together, each keeps its
own sound
filii is *fil-i-i*
eorum is *e-o-rum*
mei is *me-i*

Au, Eu, and Ay form a single sound
au as in *ouch*
eu as in *you*
ay as in *aisle*

c coming before e, ae, oe, i is pronounced ch as in *church*
cc is pronounced *T-ch*: ecce = *et-che*
sc is pronounced sh as in *shed*
c/ch in all other cases is pronounced k as in *keen*

g before e, ae, oe, i, is soft as in *generous*
g before u and o, is hard as in *governor*
gn as in *monsignor*

j is pronounced as y: major = *ma-yor*

ti before any vowel is pronounced *tsee*

th is always pronounced t as in *Thomas*

xc, as in excelsis, is pronounced *ek-shel-sis*

Every Eye Beholds You

Essential Prayers

SH'MA YISRA'EL

Sh'ma Yisra'el, Adonai Eloheinu, Adonai Ekhad.

———

Hear, O Israel, the Lord Our God, the Lord is One.

This concise creed that sums up the heart of the Jewish faith—the belief that there is only one God and the rejection of all idols—comes from Deuteronomy 6:4. Traditional Jews recite the Sh'ma four times daily: twice during the morning service, once during the evening service, and again before going to bed. For two thousand years it has been the prayer of the Jewish martyrs, and many pious Jews today hope to die reciting the Sh'ma.

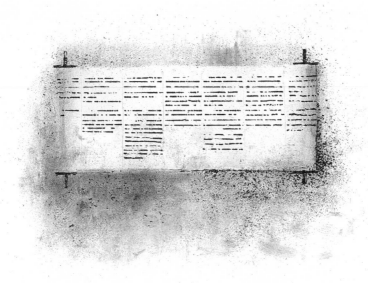

I believe in God, the Father almighty, Creator of heaven and earth; and in Jesus Christ, his only Son, our Lord; who was conceived by the Holy Spirit, born of the Virgin Mary, suffered under Pontius Pilate, was crucified, died, and was buried. He descended into hell. On the third day, he rose again from the dead. He ascended into heaven and is seated at the right hand of God, the Father almighty. From thence he shall come to judge the living and the dead. I believe in the Holy Spirit, the Holy Catholic Church, the communion of saints, the forgiveness of sins, the resurrection of the body, and the life of the world to come. Amen.

There is a legend that, after the descent of the Holy Spirit upon the Apostles at the first Pentecost, each of them pronounced an article of this creed, and it became the basis of the Christian faith. The earliest historical evidence for this creed attributed to the Apostles comes, however, from fourth-century Rome, where it was used to instruct converts. Since that time, the Church has always considered the Apostles' Creed one of the fundamental prayers every Christian must know. Even during the upheavals of the Reformation, Martin Luther, John Calvin, and Huldrych Zwingli retained it as an excellent outline of the essentials of Christian belief.

In the Beginning Was God

In the beginning was God,
Today is God,
Tomorrow will be God.
Who can make an image of God?
He has no body.
He is a word which comes out of your mouth.
That word! It is no more,
It is past, and it still lives!
So is God.

The Pygmies of the Congo recite this prayer as a type of creed that describes God as an eternal spirit. Christians will notice that it echoes the opening of Saint John's Gospel, which follows.

Beginning of Saint John's Gospel

In the beginning was the Word,
and the Word was with God,
and the Word was God.
The same was in the beginning with God.
All things were made by him;
and without him was not any thing made.
In him was life; and the life was the light of men.
And the light shineth in the darkness;
and the darkness comprehended it not.
There was a man sent from God, whose name was John.
The same came for a witness, to bear witness of the Light,
that all men through him might believe.
He was not that Light, but was sent to bear witness of that Light.
That was the true Light,
which lighteth every man that cometh into the world.
He was in the world,
and the world was made by him,
and the world knew him not.
He came unto his own,
and his own received him not.
But as many as received him,
to them gave he power
to become sons of God,
even to them that believe on his name:
Which were born,
not of blood, nor of the will of the flesh,
nor of the will of man,
but of God.

And the Word was made flesh,

and dwelt among us,

(and we beheld his glory,

the glory as of the only begotten

of the Father,)

full of grace and truth.

John 1:1-14

This prologue to the Gospel of Saint John is the most splendid work of early Christian poetry. The prologue summarizes the theme of John's gospel: Whoever accepts Jesus Christ as the Son of God (the Word made flesh) becomes a child of God. And since only Christ the Son has seen God the Father, he is the only one who can reveal God's truth and bring God's grace to the world.

THE LORD'S PRAYER

IN ARAMAIC

Aboon dabashmaya,

nethkadash shamak,

tetha malkoothak,

newe tzevyanak aykan dashmaya af bara.

Hav lan lakma dsoonkanan yamanawashbook lan,

kavine aykana daf hanan shabookan

lhayavine oolow talahn lanesyana.

Ela fatsan men beesha.

IN GREEK

Páter imón o en tis ouranís,

agiasthíto to ónoma Sou,

elthéto I Vasilía Sou,

genithíto to thelimá Sou,

os en ouranó ke epi tis gis.

Ton árton imón ton epioúsion dos imín símeron.

Ke áfes imín ta ofilímata imón,

os ke imís afíemen tis ofilétes imon.

Ke mi isenéngkis imás is pirasmón,

alla ríse imás apó tou poniroú.

IN LATIN (PATER NOSTER)

Pater noster, qui es in coelis,

sanctificetur nomen tuum.

Adveniat regnum tuum,

fiat voluntas tua, sicut in coelo et in terra.

Panem nostrum quotidianum da nobis hodie,

et dimitte nobis debita nostra,

sicut et nos dimittimus debitoribus nostris.

Et ne nos inducas in tentationem,

sed libera nos a malo.

CATHOLIC AND ORTHODOX VERSION

Our Father, who art in heaven, hallowed be thy name. Thy kingdom come, thy will be done on earth as it is in heaven. Give us this day our daily bread, and forgive us our trespasses as we forgive those who trespass against us. And lead us not into temptation, but deliver us from evil. Amen.

PROTESTANT VERSION

Our Father, which art in heaven, hallowed be thy name. Thy kingdom come, thy will be done in earth as it is in heaven. Give us this day our daily bread. And forgive us our debts, as we forgive our debtors. And lead us not into temptation, but deliver us from evil: For thine is the kingdom, and the power, and the glory, for ever. Amen.

The Lord's Prayer, which Jesus taught his apostles, is found in two versions in the gospels: Matthew 6:9-13 and Luke 11:2-4. Matthew's version is the one used universally by Christians. The distinctive final sentence that concludes the Protestant version was a common doxology, or conclusion, that Jews of the first century C.E. added to their prayers. From the text of the Lord's Prayer found in the Didache, the oldest Christian liturgical book (c. 100 C.E.), we know that the earliest Christian congregations adopted this custom. The doxology is not found, however, in the oldest and most authoritative versions of Matthew's and Luke's gospels.

From the earliest days of the Christian Church, the Lord's Prayer was recited at baptisms, and in the sixth century, Pope Saint Gregory the Great decreed that it should be said over the consecrated bread and wine before Communion was distributed. Both of these traditions survive today among many Christian denominations.

THE TRISAGION

Agios o Theos. Agios ischyros. Agios athanatos, eleison imas.

———

O Holy God. O Holy Mighty One. O Holy Immortal One, have mercy on us.

In the Eastern Orthodox Church, this ancient invocation of Christ is a regular feature of the liturgy. In the Roman Catholic Church, it is solemnly chanted on Good Friday as the congregation goes forward to kiss the cross.

Tradition says that during a procession through the streets of Constantinople in 434 C.E., a boy named Acacius was caught up to Heaven and heard the angels singing this hymn around God's throne. Returning to earth, he taught it to the Patriarch Proclus.

Whatever the origins of the hymn, it is first mentioned in the documents of the Council of Chalcedon (451 C.E.). The name, Trisagion, is Greek for "thrice holy."

AVE MARIA

Ave Maria, gratia plena, Dominus tecum. Benedicta tu in mulieribus, et benedictus fructus ventris tui, Jesu. Sancta Maria, Mater Dei, ora pro nobis peccatoribus, nunc et in hora mortis nostrae. Amen.

THE HAIL MARY

Hail Mary, full of grace, the Lord is with thee. Blessed art thou among women, and blessed is the fruit of thy womb, Jesus. Holy Mary, Mother of God, pray for us sinners, now and at the hour of our death. Amen.

The Hail Mary is the most popular prayer among Roman Catholics and more often than not the first one a Catholic child learns. The first sentence is the Archangel Gabriel's greeting to Mary at the Annunciation (Luke 1:28). The second sentence is Elizabeth's exclamation when Mary came to visit her (Luke 1:42). These two gospel verses were being recited together as a distinct prayer by Christians in the east by the sixth century. The name of Jesus was added in the thirteenth century. The prayer's final sentence came into general use in the sixteenth century.

THE JESUS PRAYER

Lord Jesus Christ, Son of the living God, have mercy upon me.

This ancient prayer is known to almost every Christian denomination, but it enjoys a special vitality among Eastern Orthodox Christians. The prayer comes out of the tradition of the first monasteries, which appeared in the Egyptian desert in the fourth century. There, the Desert Fathers urged monks to pray without ceasing, and this short prayer is one of the brief devotional formulas that developed in those ancient religious communities. It became preferred to all others because it invoked the Holy Name of Jesus. While the earliest text of the Jesus Prayer dates from the sixth century, it echoes two almost identical prayers in Luke's gospel: the cry of the blind men, "Jesus, thou Son of David, have mercy upon me" (Luke 18:38) and the prayer of the penitent tax collector, "O God be merciful to me a sinner" (Luke 18:13). Among Eastern Orthodox Christians, the Jesus Prayer is repeated over and over with the hope that it will cease to be simply a prayer of the lips and become a prayer spoken by the mind and the heart.

The First Principle of Islam

La ilaha ill-Allah, Muhammad-ur-rasool ullah.

———

There is no god but God and Muhammad is the
Messenger of God.

Declaration of the Oneness of God
(the creed of islam)

La ilaha ill-Allahu wahdahu la sharika lahu, lahul
mulku wa lahul hamdu, Yuhyi wa Yumeetu, biyadihil-
khairu, wa huwa 'ala kulli shai-in Qadeer.

———

There is none worthy of worship but God: He is One
and has no partner; His is the Kingdom [of the whole
universe], and unto Him is due all Praise; He gives life
and He causes death: In His hand is all good, and He
has power over all things.

The fundamental principle of Islam is that there is no god but God and
Muhammad is his Messenger. There are, however, other declarations of faith that
the devout Muslim recites.

THE CALL TO PRAYER (AZAN)

Allahu Akbar!

——

God is Greater!

Ash-hadu an la ilaha ill-Allah.

——

I bear witness that there is none worthy of being
worshipped except God.

Ash-hadu anna Muhammad-ar-rasoolullah.

——

I bear witness that Muhammad is the Messenger of God.

Hayya 'alas-Salah.

——

Come to Prayer.

Hayya 'alal-falah.

——

Come to Success.

Allahu Akbar.

——

God is Greater.

Five times a day, the muezzin, or crier, faces the Ka'ba shrine in Mecca and in a loud
voice calls the faithful of Islam to prayer. By tradition, the first line is repeated four
times, the second twice, the third twice. "Come to prayer" is said twice with only the
face turned to the right; "Come to Success" is said twice with only the face turned
to the left. The call ends with the final "God is Greater" proclaimed twice.

Al-Fatihah (The Opening)

Bismillah-i-Rahman-ir-Rahim.
Alhamdu lillahi
Rabbil-'aalameen ar-Rahman-ir-Rahim,
Maliki yaum-id-deen,
iyyakt na'-budu wa iyyaka nasta-'een;
ihdinas-sirat-al-mustaqeema
sirat-alla-zeena an'amta 'alaihim
ghairil maghdoobi 'alaihim wal-lad-dalleen. Ameen!

———

In the Name of God, the Beneficent, the Merciful.
Praise be to God, Lord of the Worlds,
The Beneficent, the Merciful.
Owner of the Day of Judgment,
Thee [alone] we worship; Thee [alone] we ask for help.
Show us the straight path,
The path of those whom Thou hast favored;
Not [the path] of those who earn Thine anger nor of those
who go astray. Amen.

The Qur'an begins with this most ancient of all Islamic prayers, and so it is most often referred to simply as "The Opening." It is an essential devotional element of Muslim worship, whether in public or in private, and is even recited at business transactions to seal a solemn contract. No one knows when Muhammad was first inspired to recite this prayer, but it is known that by 612 C.E., the Messenger and his small band of followers in Mecca were using it. Christians often call this the Lord's Prayer of Islam, and there are verses that echo the prayer Jesus taught his disciples.

Subhanak-Allahumma wa bihamdika wa tabarakasmuka wa ta'ala jadduka wa la ilaha ghairuka.

———

All Glory be to Thee, O God! and Praise be to Thee; blessed is Thy Name and exalted Thy Majesty; and there is none worthy of worship besides Thee.

A'oozu billahi minash-shaitanir-rajeem.

———

I betake myself to God for refuge from the accursed Satan.

Bismillah-i-Rahman-ir-Raheem.

———

[I begin] in the Name of God, the Beneficent, the Merciful.

Qul huw-Allahu Ahad, Allahus-Samad, lam yalid wa lam yoolad, wa lam yakun lahoo kufuwan ahad.

———

He is God, the One—God, the eternally besought of all! He begets not, nor is He begotten. And there is none comparable unto Him.

Subhana Rabbiyal-'Azeem

———

How glorious is my Lord, the Great!

Allahumma salli 'ala sayyidina Muhammadin wa 'ala ali sayyidina Muhammadin kama sallaita 'ala sayyidina Ibrahima wa 'ala ali sayyidina Ibrahim innaka Hamidun Majeed.

———

O God! Shower Thy blessings on our leader Muhammad and his descendants as Thou showeredest Thy blessings on our leader Abraham and his descendants; verily, Thou art the Praiseworthy, the Glorious.

The second principle of Islam calls upon devout Muslims to pray five times a day. These prayers are from the daily obligatory prayers each Muslim must offer. Muslims who ignore this obligation are considered unbelievers.

UNIVERSAL TOLERANCE

My heart is capable of every form,
a cloister of the monk, a temple for idols,
a pasture for gazelles, the votary's Ka'ba,
the tables of the Torah, the Qu'ran.
Love is the creed I hold: wherever turn
His camels, love is still my creed and faith.

Among the Sufis, the mystic Ibn 'Arabi (1165-1240) is known as the *shaikh al-akbar*, the greatest master. This personal creed is the most famous of his works and defines the Sufi ideal of universal tolerance for all religious traditions: Christian, polytheist, animist, Islamic, and Jewish.

HINDU MANTRAS

Om namu Shivaya om.

———

Hail to the Name of Shiva.

Om namu bhagavate Vasudevaya om.

———

Hail to the worshipful Lord Vishnu.

Hindus regard "om" as the most sacred Sanskrit syllable. The sound is said to be a direct manifestation of the divine, so it begins and ends all mantras. As one repeats the mantra—in these cases praising the gods Shiva and Vishnu—the goal is to unite the self with the mantra and become one with its spiritual power.

The Gayatri

Om bhur bhuvah svah om.

The adorable glory of Savitri, Deva, we contemplate;

may he arouse our intellect.

To Savitri, Deva, with our intellect, desiring power,

we pray for the gift of grace.

Savitri, Deva, wise men adore with rituals and noble hymns,

inspired by their intellect.

Rig-Veda III, 62, 10-12

This Hindu mantra, a hymn to the solar god Savitri, is considered the most sacred part of the Vedas. The Sanskrit mantra, "Om bhur bhuvah svah om," consists of sacred sounds that call forth spiritual energies. The precise meaning of these sounds has been lost, but most scholars believe they signify the tripartite cosmos of Hinduism: earth, atmosphere, and heaven.

At the initiation ceremony when men of the three upper castes are invested with the sacred thread, the brahman (a high-caste person who is also, usually, a priest) whispers this prayer in each man's ear. The prayer is repeated at all Hindu rituals and is greatly loved by believers (although tradition forbids any but the three highest castes to recite it). Among Hindus, ignorance of divine truth is deplorable, so in this essential mantra they beg the sun god to enlighten their minds and draw their hearts toward the sacred wisdom revealed in the Vedas.

The title "Deva" refers to the gods, also known as the Shining Ones, or the Divine Manifestations. But a Deva is only one facet or emanation of the Ultimate Being. Throughout the centuries, Hindu sages have coined a host of terms to define the essential character of the Ultimate Being: Aksharam, the Indestructible, the Eternal; Ekamn, the One; Sat or Tat Sat, the Ultimate Reality; Brahma, the Divine Essence; Atma, the Oversoul; and Om, an indefinable mystic term.

Who Is the Deity?

In the beginning was the Divinity in his splendor,
manifested as the sole Lord of creation,
and he upheld the earth and the heavens.
Who is the Deity we shall worship with our offerings?

It is he who bestows life-force and vigor,
whose guidance all men invoke, the Devas invoke,
whose shadow is immortal life—and death.
Who is the Deity we shall worship with our offerings?

It is he who by his greatness became
the one King of the breathing and the seeing,
who is the Lord of man and bird and beast.
Who is the Deity we shall worship with our offerings?

Lord of creation! no other than thee
pervades all these that have come into being.
May that be ours for which our prayers rise,
may we be masters of many treasures!

Rig-Veda X, 121

The Hindu god Hiranyagarbha is manifested through the glory of creation, in contrast with the Aksharam, the ineffable god who has no physical manifestation.

She shines upon a white lotus arisen from the water, pervading the world. She holds in her hands scissors, a sword, a skull, and a blue lotus. Her ornaments are snakes in the form of a zone, earrings, a garland, armlets, bracelets, anklets. She has three red eyes, fearful tawny tresses, a beautiful girdle, fearful teeth. Round the hips she wears the skin of a panther. She bears a diadem made of bleached bones. One should meditate on Tara, the mother of the three worlds seated on the heart of a corpse, her face resplendent with the power of the Never-decaying.

Tara is a goddess venerated both by Hindus and Tibetan Buddhists. Among the Buddhists, she is a goddess of infinite mercy, but as this hymn makes clear, the Hindus consider Tara a terrifying deity. In Hindu iconography, she is always portrayed with snakes in her hair and twining around her four arms. In one hand, she holds a human head, and in another a cup of blood, the life force of the world, which she drinks whenever she is angry.

Buddhist Mantras

Om mani padme om.

———

All hail the Jewel in the Lotus.

Namu myo ho renge kyo.

———

Homage to the Lotus Sutra.

Namu Amida Butsu.

———

Hail to the Amida Buddha.

"Om mani padme om" is the most famous of all the Buddhist mantras. It invokes the Enlightened Buddha under his title "Jewel in the Lotus." Repeating this mantra is believed to move closer to spiritual enlightenment.

"Namu myo ho renge kyo" was developed by Nichiren, the thirteenth-century Japanese Buddhist teacher. Nichiren considered that of all the Buddhist scriptures, the Lotus Sutra was the embodiment of all truth, and that chanting these five words from it unites one with the sutra and allows one to receive all of its benefits.

"Namu Amida Butsu" is the mantra of the Japan's Pure Land Buddhist sect. Believers chant the mantra relying on the compassion of Amida Buddha to grant them an afterlife in Paradise—the Pure Land.

TI-SARANA-GAMANA (TAKING THE THREE REFUGES)

Veneration to the Blessed One, the Enlightened One,
the Perfectly Enlightened One:
To the Buddha, the [chosen] resort I go.
To the Dharma, the [chosen] resort I go.
To the Sangha, the [chosen] resort I go.
For the second time to the Buddha, the [chosen] resort I go.
For the second time to the Dharma, the [chosen] resort I go.
For the second time to the Sangha, the [chosen] resort I go.
For the third time to the Buddha, the [chosen] resort I go.
For the third time to the Dharma, the [chosen] resort I go.
For the third time to the Sangha, the [chosen] resort I go.

And now I betake myself, Lord, to the Blessed One as my
refuge, to the Truth, and to the Order. May the Blessed One
accept me as a disciple, as one who, from this day forth, as long
as life endures, has taken refuge in them.

The Mahayana tradition of the Buddhist faith is guided by three components
traditionally called the "The Three Jewels": Buddha (the Enlightened One) himself; the Dharma, which are the teachings of the Buddha; and the Sangha, which
is the Buddhist Order or community of believers. The most fundamental act of
Mahayana Buddhist worship is to recognize, embrace, and venerate these three
essential elements of the faith.

Prayer to the Supreme Dual God

Lord, our master:

she of the jade skirt,

he who shines like a sun of jade.

A male has been born,

sent here by our mother, our father,

Lord of Duality, Lady of Duality,

he who dwells in the nine heavens,

he who dwells in the place of duality.

You live in heaven;

you uphold the mountain,

Anahuac is in your hands.

Awaited, you art always everywhere;

you are invoked, you are prayed to.

Your glory, your fame is sought.

You live in heaven;

Anahuac is in your hands.

Our Master, the Lord of the Close Vicinity,

thinks and does what He wishes; He determines,

He amuses himself.

As He wishes, so will it be.

In the palm of his hand He has us; at His will

He shifts us around.

We shift around; like marbles we roll; He rolls

us around endlessly.

We are but toys to Him; He laughs at us.

Rise, array yourself, stand on your feet,
partake of the pleasure of the beautiful place,
the home of your mother, your father, the Sun.
Good fortune, pleasure and happiness are there.
Go forth, follow your mother, your father, the Sun.

The Toltecs worshiped Ometeotl, the Supreme Dual God, a single deity who blended the characteristics of both a father god and a mother goddess. It is thought that Ometeotl evolved from a unification of sun and earth cults, forming a single god from a father god who begets all life and a goddess who is a universal mother.

This is a rather sophisticated prayer, perhaps even a creed that defines the nature of the Dual God and ponders whether human actions are an exercise of free will or part of the mysterious designs of Ometeotl.

TWO PRAYERS OF THE GHOST DANCE

ANI'QU NE'CHAWU'NANI'

> Father, have pity on me,
> Father, have pity on me;
> I am crying for thirst,
> I am crying for thirst;
> All is gone—I have nothing to eat,
> All is gone—I have nothing to eat.

MAKA' SITO'MANIYAN UKIYE

> The whole world is coming,
> A nation is coming, a nation is coming,
> The Eagle has brought the message to the tribe.
> The father says so, the father says so.
> Over the whole earth they are coming.
> The buffalo are coming, the buffalo are coming,
> The Crow has brought the message to the tribe,
> The father says so, the father says so.

In the 1880s, when the Native American people were all but entirely defeated, Wovoka, an Indian mystic, began to preach the messianic cult of the Ghost Dance among the Plains tribes. Wovoka taught that ecstatic singing and dancing would raise the dead, bring back the vanished buffalo, make believers impervious to bullets, and drive the white men out of the country forever.

The first chant is from the Arapaho and invokes the Father-Messiah who will come to save the tribes. It is possible that this prayer was influenced by the Christian Lord's Prayer.

The second chant is Sioux and sums up the faith of the Ghost Dancers. The Sioux's two sacred birds, the Eagle and the Crow, deliver the good news of redemption to the tribe.

'Tis the gift to be simple, 'tis the gift to be free,

'Tis the gift to come down where we ought to be.

And when we find ourselves in the place just right

'Twill be in the valley of love and delight.

When true simplicity is gain'd

To bow and to bend we shall not be asham'd

To turn, turn will be our delight

'Til by turning, turning we come round right.

The Shakers were an unusual sect, founded in England by Mother Ann Lee (1736-1784), a visionary who believed she was a reincarnation of Christ. In 1774, Mother Ann brought her followers to America, where they established communities in which men and women lived as celibates. The communities became famous for their ecstatic dancing (hence their popular name, "Shakers"), their lively hymns, their industriousness, and their prosperity. At their peak in 1860, there were some six thousand Shakers in America. After the Civil War, a variety of social and economic pressures contributed to a gradual decline in the society's numbers. Today, there are only a handful of Shakers.

Mary Hazzard, an Eldress of the Shaker community in New Lebanon, New York, was blessed with the gift of superb calligraphy. Over her lifetime, she created a tremendous body of work: hymns written out in the peculiar Shaker musical notation, maps for dances, as well as inspirational drawings. This text of "Simple Gifts," perhaps the most widely known of all the Shaker hymns (thanks in part to Aaron Copland, who borrowed it for his symphonic work *Appalachian Spring*) was taken directly from one of Eldress Hazzard's manuscripts.

Ein Keilo-heinu (There Is None Like Our God)

Ein keilo-heinu, ein kado-neinu, ein k'mal-keinu, ein k'moshi-einu.

Mi kheilo-heinu, mi khado-neinu, mi kh'mal-keinu, mi kh'moshi-einu.

Nodeh leilo-heinu, nodeh lado-neinu, nodeh l'mal-keinu, nodeh l'moshi-einu.

Barukh elo-heinu, barukh ado-neinu, barukh mal-keinu, barukh moshi-einu.

Attah hu elo-heinu, attah hu ado-neinu, attah hu mal-keinu, attah hu moshi-einu.

Attah hu sheh-hiktiru avoteinu l'fanekha et k'toret hasamim.

———

There is none like our God; there is none like our Lord; there is none like our King; there is none like our Deliverer.

Who is like our God? Who is like our Lord? Who is like our King? Who is like our Deliverer?

Let us give thanks to our God; let us give thanks to our Lord; let us give thanks to our King; let us give thanks to our Deliverer.

Blessed be our God; blessed be our Lord; blessed be our King; blessed be our Deliverer.

Thou art our God; thou art our Lord; thou art our King; thou art our Deliverer.

Thou art he to whom our fathers offered the fragrant incense.

Sephardic Jews sing this prayer daily, while Ashkenazic Jews sing it toward the end of the Sabbath morning service. Since the melody is universal, Ein Keilo-heinu is one of the popular prayers from the Jewish prayer book.

ADON OLAM (MASTER OF ETERNITY)

Adon olam asher malakh, b'terem kol ye-tzir nivra.
L'eit na-asah ve-heftzo kol, azai melekh sh'mo nikra.
Ve-aharei kikhlot hakol, le-vado yimlokh nora.
Ve-hu hayah, ve-hu hoveh, ve-hu yih-yeh b'tifarah.
Ve-hu ehad ve-ein shei-ni, le-hamshil lo le-hahbirah.
B'li rei-sheet b'li takhleet, ve-lo ha-oz ve-hamisrah
Ve-hu Eili ve-hai go-ali, ve-tzur hevli b'eit tzarah
Ve-hu nisi u-manos li, m'nat kosi b'yom ekra.
B'yado afkid ruhi, b'eit ishan ve-a-irah.
Ve-im ruhi ge-viyati, Adonai li ve-lo ira.

———

He is the eternal Lord who reigned
Before any being was created.
At the time when all was made by his will,
He was at once acknowledged as King.
And at the end, when all shall cease to be,
The revered God alone shall still be King.
He was, he is, and he shall be
In glorious eternity.
He is One, and there is no other
To compare to him, to place beside him.
He is without beginning, without end;
Power and dominion belong to him.
He is my God, my living Redeemer,
My stronghold in times of distress.
He is my guide and my refuge,
My share of bliss the day I call.
To him I entrust my spirit

When I sleep and when I wake.
As long as my soul is with my body
The Lord is with me; I am not afraid.

By the standards of the Jewish liturgy, the Adon Olam is a comparatively new prayer, having been composed in the Middle Ages and included in the synagogue service in the fifteenth century. Some congregations recite this hymn of praise every morning and at the conclusion of the Saturday morning service.

A Mighty Fortress Is Our God

A mighty fortress is our God,
A bulwark never failing;
Our helper he amid the flood
Of mortal ills prevailing:
For still our ancient foe
Doth seek to work us woe;
His craft and power are great,
And, armed with cruel hate,
On earth is not his equal.

Did we in our own strength confide
Our striving would be losing;
Were not the right Man on our side,
The Man of God's own choosing.
Dost ask who that may be?
Christ Jesus, it is he;

Lord Sabbaoth his Name,

From age to age the same,

And he must win the battle.

And though this world, with devils filled,

Should threaten to undo us;

We will not fear, for God hath willed

His truth to triumph through us:

The prince of darkness grim,

We tremble not for him;

His rage we can endure,

For lo! his doom is sure,

One little word shall fell him.

That word above all earthly powers,

No thanks to them, abideth;

The Spirit and the gifts are ours

Through him who with us sideth:

Let goods and kindred go,

This mortal life also;

The body they may kill:

God's truth abideth still,

His kingdom is forever.

Martin Luther (1483-1546) was an enthusiastic student of music. After his break with Rome, he encouraged choral and congregational singing in his new worship service. He wrote lyrics (and perhaps some of the melodies) for dozens of hymns that are the core of the Lutheran hymnal. "A Mighty Fortress Is Our God," written in 1527, became the anthem of the Reformation, and by tradition it is still sung on Reformation Sunday at the end of October to commemorate the day Luther nailed his ninety-five theses to the door of the Castle Church at Wittenburg.

Hymn to the Creator

Hail, you Former,
you Shaper,
look upon us,
hear us.
Do not oppress us;
Do not turn on us,
Oh God in Heaven, Heart of Earth!
Give us our sign, our word,
on the road of day,
on the road of light,
when it is whitened,
when it is brightened.
Great be the wealth of the path,
the wealth of the road.
Give us then tranquillity and light,
tranquillity and peace;
perfect light
and perfect peace may there be.
Perfect life
and existence
give us then,
you, One Leg,
Dwarf Lightning, Green Lightning,
Dwarf Quarter Gods,
Green Quarter Gods,
Hawk, Hunter,
Majesty, Quetzal Serpent,
Bearer, Engenderer,
Xpiacoc, Xmucane,

The Grandmother of Day,
The Grandmother of Light,
as it has been whitened,
as it has been brightened.

One of the themes of the *Popol Vuh*, the sacred Mayan text written down in the sixteenth century by a Mayan convert to Christianity, is the successive creations of the world. In this hymn, set in the earliest days of human history, the Quiche people sing to their gods, begging for the blessings of light and peace. The Quarter Gods invoked in the text are the deities who rule over the four quarters of the earth.

PSALM 23

The Lord is my shepherd;
I shall not want.
He maketh me to lie down in green pastures:
he leadeth me beside the still waters.
He restoreth my soul:
he leadeth me in the paths of righteousness for his name's sake.
Yea, though I walk through the valley of the shadow of death,
I will fear no evil:
for thou art with me;
thy rod and thy staff
they comfort me.
Thou preparest a table before me
in the presence of mine enemies:
thou anointest my head with oil;
my cup runneth over.
Surely goodness and mercy shall follow me all the days of my life:
and I will dwell in the house of the Lord forever.

Undoubtedly, this is the most popular of all the psalms—particularly in the universally beloved translation of the King James Bible. As an expression of complete confidence in God, the Twenty-third Psalm has no rival. It is prayed in times of trouble and is frequently offered at funerals to console the mourners.

Prayers of the Day and of the Seasons

STUDENTS' MORNING PRAYER

O Lord God, we humbly beseech thee to direct our thoughts and prayers this day; purify our hearts from every evil and false imagination, and may no vain and worldly desires have their abode in us. Keep us from all wandering looks and ways, from an undevout mind, and careless prayers. Let the voice of thy love enter our souls, that we may study thy word with reverence and holy fear, with fervor and delight. O God, thou seest us: help us to look up unto thee; for the sake of thy Son, Jesus Christ, our Lord. Amen.

This prayer is found in an Episcopalian collection called *The Office for Special Occasions*. Although the prayer dates from about 1900, its style and vocabulary has been inspired by the sixteenth-century Anglican classic, *Book of Common Prayer*.

FOR A DAY FULL OF BLESSINGS

O sun, as you rise in the east through God's leadership,
Wash away all the evils of which I have thought throughout
the night.
Bless me, so that my enemies will not kill me and my family;
Guide me through hard work.
O God, give me mercy upon our children who are suffering:
Bring riches today as the sun rises;
Bring all fortunes to me today.

In Kenya, where this morning prayer is generally said by old men of the Abaluyia people, the sun is not a deity itself but a symbol of God's perpetual presence. This prayer includes two common petitions: protection from physical harm and an increase of material riches.

Upon awakening in the morning

I render my thanks to thee, everlasting King, who hast mercifully restored my soul within me; thy faithfulness is great.

When washing the hands

Blessed art thou, Lord our God, King of the universe, who hast sanctified us with thy commandments, and commanded us concerning the washing of hands.

When dressed

The Torah which Moses handed down to us is the heritage of the community of Jacob. May blessings rest on my head. Hear, my son, your father's instruction, and reject not your mother's teaching. The Torah shall be my trust, and the Almighty my help. God is a faithful King. Hear, O Israel, the Lord is our God, the Lord is One. Blessed be the name of his glorious majesty forever and ever. You who cling to the Lord are all alive today. For thy salvation I hope, O Lord.

My God, guard my tongue from evil, and my lips from speaking falsehood. Open my heart to thy Torah, that my soul may follow thy commands. May the words of my mouth and the meditation of my heart be pleasing before thee, O Lord, my Stronghold and my Redeemer.

At the heart of the Jewish Morning Prayer is the Sh'ma Yisra'el—Hear, O Israel—Judaism's fundamental confession of faith and the first Hebrew verse taught to Jewish children.

A Child's Morning Prayer

Heavenly Father, make us, we pray thee, such children as Jesus was, quick to obey, glad to be taught, and never afraid to speak the truth. May we hurt nobody by word or deed, but all day long be good to others, as thou, dear Lord, has been most kind to us. We ask it in the name of Jesus Christ, our Lord. Amen.

The exalted prose style of the *Book of Common Prayer*—the inspiration for almost all Anglican prayers—has been simplified somewhat in this prayer composed around 1900 especially for children.

Night Prayer

Blessed art thou, Lord our God, King of the universe, who closest my eyes in sleep, my eyelids in slumber.

May it be thy will, Lord my God and God of my fathers, to grant that I lie down in peace and that I rise again to life.

Hear, O Israel, the Lord our God, the Lord is One.

Blessed be the name of his glorious majesty forever and ever.

You shall love the Lord your God with all your heart, and with all your soul, and with all your might. And these words which I command you today shall be in your heart. You shall teach them diligently to your children, and you shall speak of them when you are sitting at home and when you go on a journey, when you lie down and when you rise up. You shall bind them for a sign on your hand, and they shall be for frontlets between your eyes. You shall inscribe them on the doorposts of your house and on your gates.

Blessed be the Lord by day; blessed be the Lord by night; blessed be the Lord when we lie down; blessed be the Lord when we rise up.

The Guardian of Israel neither slumbers nor sleeps.

Into thy hand I commit my spirit; O Lord, faithful God, thou savest me.

For thy salvation I hope, O Lord.

The Talmud teaches that every Jew ought to recite or read the Sh'ma Yisra'el—Hear, O Israel—before retiring for the night.

RABI'A'S EVENING PRAYER

O my Lord, the stars are shining and the eyes of men are closed, and kings have shut their doors and every lover is alone with his beloved, and here am I alone with Thee.

Rabi'a al-'Adawiyya (c. 717-801) was a Sufi saint and mystic who lived in Basra in what is now Iraq. Like a Christian nun, she took a vow of chastity and refused all offers of marriage. Her sanctity and her pure love for God were such that one contemporary called her "a second Mary." A biographer said that after dark, Rabi'a would go up on the roof of her house and begin her evening devotions with this prayer.

Evening Prayer of W.E.B. Du Bois

Lord of the springtime, Father of flower, field and fruit, smile on us in these earnest days when the work is heavy and the toil wearisome; lift up our hearts, O God, to the things worthwhile: sunshine and night, the dripping rain, the song of birds, books and music, and the voices of our friends. Lift up our hearts to these this night, O Father, and grant us Thy peace. Amen.

W.E.B. Du Bois (1868-1963) was a writer, educator, activist, and at one time president of the National Association for the Advancement of Colored People (NAACP). Although an agnostic and frequently a harsh critic of complacent and hypocritical Christians, Du Bois found in the literature of the Old and New Testaments themes that inspired own his writings and speeches: the importance of commitment and hard work, the willingness to take risks and endure sacrifice, the necessity of preparing oneself for great challenges in an often hostile world. Du Bois wrote these prayers in 1909 and 1910, about the time he was working to establish the NAACP, an organization he hoped would spark a new movement to liberate African Americans, in the tradition of the Abolitionists.

SLEEP CONSECRATION

I lie down tonight
With fair Mary and with her Son,
With pure-white Michael,
And with Bride beneath her mantle.

I lie down with God,
And God will lie down with me,
I will not lie down with Satan,
Nor shall Satan lie down with me.

O God of the poor,
help me this night,
Omit me not entirely
From Thy treasure-house.

For the many wounds
That I inflicted on Thee,
I cannot this night
Enumerate them.

Thou King of the blood of truth,
Do not forget me in Thy dwelling place,
Do not exact from me for my transgressions,
Do not omit me in Thine ingathering,
In Thine ingathering.

As an Exciseman, Alexander Carmichael (1832-1912) traveled throughout the Scottish Highlands and islands. Over time, he became fascinated with the Gaelic prayers, hymns, incantations, blessings, and charms he encountered among the local people. He began to record them, eventually publishing two volumes of Gaelic texts, with translations and notes, in 1900. His daughter and grandson completed his work and published four more volumes after his death.

Carmichael collected many Gaelic charms before sleep. As with so many of the texts in the *Carmina Gadelica*, the believer calls upon the protection of the Blessed Virgin Mary, the most powerful saint in Heaven; Saint Michael the Archangel, who thrust Satan and his fallen angels into Hell and is the defender of all Christians; and Saint Bride, or Brigid, the foremost female Celtic saint.

And now as we lay down to sleep, O Master, grant us repose both of body and of soul, and keep us from the dark sleep of sin and from the sensuous pleasure of the dark passions of the night. Still thou the assaults of passion; quench the fiery darts of the wicked one which are thrown insidiously at us; calm the commotions of our flesh and put away all earthly and material thoughts as we sleep. And grant us, O God, a watchful mind, chaste thoughts, a sober heart, and a gentle sleep, free from the fantasies of Satan. And raise us up again at the hour of prayer, established in thy commandments and holding steadfast within ourselves the remembrance of thy judgments. Give us the words of thy glorification, all night long, that we may praise, bless, and glorify thy most honorable and magnificent Name, O Father, Son, and Holy Spirit, now and always and for ever and ever. Amen.

O most glorious one, O ever-virgin, O blessed Theotokos, commend our prayer to thy son, our God, and entreat him to save our souls through thee.

The Father is my hope; the Son is my refuge; the Holy Spirit is my shelter. O Holy Trinity, glory to thee.

All my hope I place in thee, O Theotokos; keep me under the wing of thy care.

This Eastern Orthodox prayer is recited at Compline, the final prayer service of the day in monasteries and convents. Theotokos is the Greek word for "Mother of God" or more correctly, "God-bearer."

Two Prayers at Midnight

I

Lord, as we gather here in the middle of the night
we offer you thanksgiving
as far as our strength permits,
and so we pray:
keep safe the treasure of learning
that you set in our hearts,
place on our lips the words of your wisdom
and deliver us from all that lurks in the dark.

For yours is the greatness,
the majesty, the power and the glory,
Father, Son and Holy Spirit,
now and for ever,
to the ages of ages. Amen.

II

Almighty God, you are Lord of time
and have neither beginning nor end:
you are the redeemer of our souls,
the foundation of human reason
and guardian of our hearts;
through all that you have created
you have revealed your indescribable power;
receive, O Lord,
our supplication
even at this hour of the night,
provide fully for the needs of each one of us
and make us worthy of your goodness.

For your Name
is worthy of all honor and greatness
and is to be glorified with hymns of blessing,
Father, Son and Holy Spirit,
now and for ever,
to the ages of ages. Amen.

These two prayers come from a late eighth-century Greek manuscript of prayers for all hours of the day. In a twenty-four-hour cycle, eight liturgical services are conducted in Orthodox monastic and convent churches. Traditionally, the priest has recited these prayers before the altar in a low tone so that the congregation never heard them. To reach a wider audience of the faithful, the prayers were translated in a new, modern English edition in 1996.

PRAYER FOR USE ON SATURDAYS

On you we call, Lord God,
all-wise, all-surveying, holy,
the only true Sovereign.
You created the universe,
you watch over all that exists.
Those that lie in darkness,
overshadowed by death,
you guide into the right road, the safe road.
Your will is that all men should be saved
and come to knowledge of the truth.

With one voice we offer you
praise and thanksgiving;
full-hearted, full-throated we sing to you
the hymn you have a right to at this hour.
In your mercy you called to us
(holy the calling!),
taught us and trained us,
gave understanding, wisdom, truth to us,
life eternal.

You bought us back
with the pure and precious blood
of your only Son,
freed us from lies and error,
from bitter enslavement,
released us from the Devil's clutches
and gave us the glory of freedom.
We were dead and you renewed the life
of our souls and bodies in the Spirit.
We were soiled and you made us quite spotless again.

We pray you, merciful Father,
God from whom all encouragement comes,
give us strength to act as befits men with such a
vocation,
such calling to worship, such newness of life.
We mean to observe the sacred commands
of the divine law;
we long to come closer to you, closer today,
long to have light from you, light to know you and
serve you.

We pray you, give us the strength
to do all this with a will.
Do not think of the sins we have committed
or of those we still commit.
Put out of your mind the failings we give way to
night and day.
Do not impute our offenses to us,
whether we did them on purpose
or whether we could not help them,
Remember, Lord,
that men are apt to make slips;
we are a spineless race, given to blundering:
think of our build, our limitations.
Our skins may be sound, but there are sores
underneath.

O God, you are well disposed to us:
give us the strength of your support.
Give us encouragement, give the light that goes with it.
Make us live by the dogmas of the faith
preached by your holy apostles
and the high teaching of the gospels
of our Savior, Jesus Christ.

A fourth-century Egyptian papyrus records this magnificent prayer, which
appears to have been recited in the evening to mark the ending of the week. The
consistent use of the plural leads one to believe that this was meant to be said by
a congregation rather than as a private devotion.

MYSTICAL POEM OF RUMI (41)

Come, for today is for us a day of festival; henceforward joy and pleasure are on the increase. Clap hands, say, "Today is all happiness"; from the beginning it was a manifestly fine day.

Who is there in this world like our Friend? Who has seen such a festival in a hundred cycles?

Earth and heaven are filled with sugar; in every direction sugarcane has sprouted.

The roar of that pearl-scattering sea has arrived; the world is full of waves, and the sea is invisible.

Muhammad has returned from the Ascension; Jesus has arrived from the fourth heaven.

Every coin which is not of this place is counterfeit; every wine which is not of the cup of the Soul is impure.

～

Now I have fallen asleep and stretched out my feet, since I have realized that good fortune has drawn me on.

Jalal al-Din Rumi (1207-73 C.E.) is among the most renowned Persian mystical poets. He was a conventional Muslim theologian until, in 1244, at age thirty-seven, he met a wandering dervish named Shams al-Din. Rumi became fascinated with this impassioned holy man and was himself converted to an emotionally intense form of Islam. This mystical poem conveys the rapture of the poet.

PRAYER AT THE NEW MOON

May you be for us a moon of joy and happiness. Let the
young become strong and the grown man maintain his
strength, the pregnant woman be delivered and the
woman who has given birth suckle her child. Let the
stranger come to the end of his journey and those who
remain at home dwell safely in their houses. Let the
flocks that go to feed in the pastures return happily.
May you be a moon of harvest and of calves. May you
be a moon of restoration and of good health.

The new moon was once widely celebrated throughout Africa with special cere-
monies and prayers. The Mensa people of Ethiopia, hoping they will enjoy all the
good things of life in the next month, offer this prayer at the new moon.

To the New Moon

Hail to thee, thou new moon,
Guiding jewel of gentleness!
I am bending to thee my knee,
I am offering thee my love.

I am bending to thee my knee,
I am giving thee my hand,
I am lifting to thee mine eye,
O new moon of the seasons.

Hail to thee, thou new moon,
Joyful maiden of my love!
Hail to thee, thou new moon,
Joyful maiden of the graces!

Thou art traveling in thy course,
Thou art steering the full tides;
Thou art illumining to us thy face,
O new moon of the seasons.

Thou queen-maiden of guidance,
Thou queen-maiden of good fortune,
Thou queen-maiden my beloved,
Thou new moon of the seasons!

Alexander Carmichael found many instances of moon worship throughout the Scottish islands. On the island of Barra, even into the twentieth century, it was the custom for women to curtsy or genuflect when they saw the new moon.

Prayer at the "Yearly Killing" Festival

Thou, O Tsui-goab [God]!
Father of our fathers,
Thou our Father!
Let the thundercloud stream!
Let our flocks live!
Let us also live, please!

I am so very weak indeed
From thirst,
From hunger!
Let me eat field fruits!
Art thou not our Father?
The Father of the fathers,
Thou Tsui-goab?

O that we may praise thee!
That we may bless!
Thou Father of the fathers!
Thou our Lord!
Thou, oh, Tsui-goab!

Just before the beginning of the rainy season, the Nama people of South Africa gather together and each family offers a sacrifice of milk, a pregnant ewe, or a cow. They celebrate this "yearly killing" with songs and dances and prayers to God for plenty of rain.

FOR LIFE TO MY PEOPLE

The edges of the years have met, I take sheep and
new yams and give you that you may eat.
Life to me.
Life to this my Ashanti people.
Women who cultivate the farms, when they do so,
grant that the food comes forth in abundance.
Do not allow any illness to come.

In Ghana, the king of the Ashanti people offers this prayer on the feast day of
purification, when the spirits of the dead kings are honored with sacrifices of
sheep, wine, and yams. The Ashanti hope the dead will accept the lives of animals
and spare the lives of people.

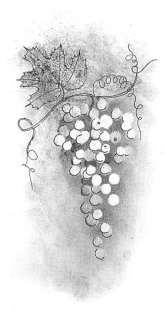

Let every devout and God-loving man enjoy this fair and radiant festival. Let every grateful servant enter into the joy of the Lord. Let him that has labored in fasting, receive now his reward.

Let him that has toiled from the first hour, receive his recompense. Let him that has come after the third hour, celebrate with thanksgiving. Let him that has arrived after the sixth hour, entertain no doubt, for he shall suffer no loss whatever. Let him that has delayed until the ninth hour, approach without hesitation. Let him that has tarried until the eleventh hour, be not alarmed by his tardiness. For the Lord is gracious, and will receive the last even as the first; he gives rest unto him who comes at the eleventh hour even as unto him who has toiled from the first.

He has mercy upon the last, he rewards the first; he gives to this one, and he bestows upon that one; he accepts the deeds, and welcomes the thought; he honors the acts, and commends the intention. Therefore, enter into the joy of our Lord all of you, and receive your reward, both the first and likewise the second.

Rich and poor, dance together. Sober and slothful, celebrate the festival. Both you that have fasted and have not, rejoice today. The table is richly laden, share it all. The food is plentiful, let no one go hungry away. Enjoy the festival of faith, all of you. Receive the riches of goodness, all of you. Let no one bewail his poverty, for the common kingdom has been revealed.

Let no one weep for his iniquities, for pardon has shone from the grave. Let no one fear death, for the Savior's death has set us free. He abolished death by enduring it. He despoiled Hades by descending into his kingdom. He angered him by allowing him to taste of his own flesh. Isaiah prophesied it when he cried, Hades was angered when he encountered thee in the lower regions. He was angered, for he was frustrated. He was angered, for he was overthrown. He was angered, for he was annihilated. He was angered, for he was fettered in chains. He was angered, for he was slain.

He received a body, and faced God. He received earth, and encountered heaven. He received the visible, and was overthrown by the invisible.

O Death, where is thy sting? O Hades, where is thy pride?

Christ is risen, and thou art abolished. Christ is risen, and the demons are fallen. Christ is risen, and the Angels rejoice. Christ is risen, and life reigns. Christ is risen, and not one dead remains in the grave.

For Christ, who rose from the dead, has become the leader and reviver of those who have fallen asleep. To him be glory and dominion unto ages of ages. Amen.

His remarkable eloquence won for Saint John (c. 347-407 C.E.) the title "Chrysostom," which means "golden-mouthed." And certainly John's rhetorical gifts are displayed in this Easter prayer.

Two motifs are especially striking. In a brilliant adaptation of Christ's parable of the laborers, John assures us that those who put off their spiritual preparation for Easter until the last minute are as welcome to celebrate the festival as those who kept the fast strictly throughout all forty days of Lent. And drawing upon his classical education, John imagines Christ overthrowing Hades, the pagan god of the underworld.

Prayers of Yearning for the Divine

A Prayer of Saint Teresa of Avila

Oh my Delight, Lord of all created things and my God! How long will I have to wait to see your presence? What help can You give to one who finds so little here on earth to be able to find some rest apart from You? O long life! O painful life! O life that is not really life! O lonesome loneliness! There is no relief! When, Lord, when? How long? What will I do, my God, what will I do? Can I perchance desire not to desire You? O my God and my Creator, Who wounds but does not offer any medicine; you strike but no wound is seen; You kill, leaving even more life. Finally, my Lord, You do as You will since You are all-powerful. Well then, my God, do You desire that so despicable a worm suffer such conflicts? Let it be so, my God, since you want it so, and I do not but what You want.

But alas, alas, my Creator, for great pain makes one complain and say things for which there is no remedy until You send one! And my imprisoned soul wishes its freedom, desiring not to deviate in the slightest from what You want. Resolve, my Glory, that its pain be increased or that it be entirely remedied. O death, death, I know not who fears you, because life is in you! But who will not fear having wasted part of it in not loving its God? And since I am such a one, what do I ask and what do I desire? Perchance the punishment that I have so well merited for my faults? Do not permit it, my God, because it cost You dearly to redeem me.

O my soul! Allow the will of God to be done; this is very fitting for you. Serve God and hope in His mercy, so that He will grant a remedy for your pain, when penance for your faults will gain some pardon for them; do not seek enjoyment without suffering.

O my true Lord and my King! Even for this I am not fit, if Your sovereign hand and greatness do not favor me, but with this I can do all things.

This prayer comes from a collection of meditations or inspirations that the great Spanish mystic Saint Teresa of Avila (1515-1582) experienced after receiving Holy Communion. She recorded them privately, and they went unpublished until 1588, six years after her death. These prayers reflect the great themes of Saint Teresa's mystical writings: her intimacy with God, her fervent love for Christ and longing to be with him always, and her profound devotion to Christ present in the Eucharist.

A Prayer before Holy Communion

My heart is wounded, O Master;
my zeal for you has melted me away;
my love for you has changed me;
my utter devotion has bound me to you.
let me be filled with your flesh;
let me be satiated
with your living and deifying blood;
let me enjoy whatever is good;
let me delight in your divinity;
let me become worthy to meet you
as you come in glory,
and let me be caught up by the clouds,
in the air,
together with all your chosen ones,
that I may praise, worship, and glorify you
in thanksgiving and doxology,
together with your Father
who is without beginning,
and your all-holy,
good and life-creating Spirit,
now and ever and unto the ages of ages. Amen.

Saint John of Damascus (676-760) served as minister of Christian affairs in Muslim-occupied Syria, a post his father held before him. In time, he gave up his career as a civil servant and entered a monastery in Jerusalem. Saint John wrote innumerable hymns and prayers that are still used in churches of the East and West, but he is most famous for his treatise against the iconoclasts, "On the Holy Images."

A Vision of God

In the market, in the cloister—only God I saw.
In the valley and on the mountain—only God I saw.
Him I have seen beside me oft in tribulation;
In favor and in fortune—only God I saw.
In prayer and fasting, in praise and contemplation,
In the religion of the Prophet—only God I saw.
Neither soul nor body, accident nor substance,
Qualities nor causes—only God I saw.
Like a candle I was melting in His fire
Amidst the flames outflashing—only God I saw.
Myself with mine own eyes I saw most clearly,
But when I looked with God's eyes—only God I saw.
I passed away into nothingness, I vanished,
And lo, I was the All-living—only God I saw.

The Sufi mystic Baba Kuhi of Shiraz looks forward to the moment when neither the business of the world, nor the beauty of nature, nor the disputes of theologians ("accident nor substance, Qualities nor causes") will mean anything to him because his individuality will have been dissolved and immersed in union with God.

Yearning and Love for God

My heart is dying though it lives.
I played day and night with my comrades, and now I am greatly afraid.

So high is my Lord's palace, my heart trembles to mount its
stairs: yet I must not be shy, if I would enjoy His love.
My heart must cleave to my Lover: I must withdraw my veil,
and meet him with all my body.
Mine eyes must perform the ceremony of the lamps of love.

~

The shadows of evening fall thick and deep, and the darkness
of love envelops the body and the mind.
Open the window to the west, and be lost in the sky of love;
Drink the sweet honey that steeps the petals of the lotus of
the heart.

~

This day is dear to me above all other days, for today the
Beloved Lord is a guest in my house;
My chamber and my courtyard are beautiful with his presence;
My songs sing His Name, and they are become lost in His
great beauty: I wash His feet, and I look upon His Face and I
lay before him as a man offering my body, my mind, and all
that I have.

What a day of gladness is that day in which my Beloved,
who is my treasure, comes to my house. All evils fly from
my heart when I see my Lord.
My love has touched Him; my heart is longing for the Name
which is Truth.

Kabir (1440-1518) was a mystic whose Hinduism was strongly influenced by
India's Islamic Mughal culture. He believed that no formal set of doctrines could
comprehend the mystery of God—only mystical experience would come close to
accomplishing that goal.

LOVE DIVINE, ALL LOVES EXCELLING

Love divine, all loves excelling,
Joy of heaven, to earth come down,
Fix in us thy humble dwelling,
All thy faithful mercies crown!
Jesu, thou art all compassion,
Pure, unbounded love thou art;
Visit us with thy salvation!
Enter every trembling heart.

Come almighty to deliver,
Let us all thy grace receive;
Suddenly return, and never,
Never more thy temples leave.
Thee we would be always blessing,
Serve thee as thy hosts above,
Pray, and praise thee without ceasing,
Glory in thy perfect love.

Finish then thy new creation,
Pure and spotless let us be;
Let us see thy great salvation
Perfectly restored in thee;
Changed from glory into glory,
Till in heaven we take our place,
Till we cast our crowns before thee,
Lost in wonder, love and praise.

Of the fifty-five hundred hymns by Charles Wesley (1707-1788), this remains one of his most popular. Wesley's goal was always to teach the truths of the

Methodist faith through his hymns. In "Love Divine," he blends a prayer for Christ to take up spiritual residence in the hearts of believers, with a prayer that Christ will hasten the day of the Second Coming, "suddenly return," and establish his New Heaven and New Earth.

A PRAYER OF THOMAS À KEMPIS

O most sweet and loving Lord, whom I now devoutly wish to receive, you know my weaknesses and my needs. You know how many bad habits and vices I have. You know how often I am burdened, tempted, shaken and stained by sin. I come to you for healing. I pray to you for comfort and support. I speak to you, who know all things, to whom all my inmost thoughts are evident. You alone can adequately comfort me and help me. You know what good things I need most, and you know how poor I am in virtue.

Look! I stand before you poor and naked, asking your grace and imploring your mercy. Feed me, for I am hungry. Inflame my coldness with the fire of your love. Illuminate my blindness with the light of your presence. Make all that leads me from you not worth thinking about. Make me forget it all. Lift up my heart to you in heaven, and let me not wander aimlessly about the world. From now on, you will be my only delight, for you alone are my food and drink, my love and joy, my sweetness and my whole good.

Oh, that by your presence you would set me fully on fire, totally consume me and transform me into you, so that through the grace of inner union and by melting in love's flames I would become one spirit with you. Do not leave me hungry and thirsty, but treat me mercifully as you have so often and so admirably treated your saints. How wonderful it would be if I were burned and wholly consumed for you, since you are a fire always burning and never consuming, a love that purifies the heart and enlightens the mind.

This prayer comes from the last book of the renowned mystical work *The Imitation of Christ*, by the Dutch priest Blessed Thomas à Kempis (c. 1379-1471). The book teaches that nothing is more certain than God's love for humankind, and nothing is more rewarding than intimate conversation with Christ. Since 1503, when the first English translation of it was published, *The Imitation of Christ* has never been out of print.

An Anabaptist Hymn

The Father has chosen us out of grace
And has not rejected us
Let us then, when our time comes
Receive the reward with joy.

Prepare us for Communion
Through Christ your beloved son
Clothe us with your Spirit
Protect us from suffering and death.

If we would eat this meal
Who serves us at the table?
As all hearts know, this is done
By the one who made atonement for sin.

Blessed are those invited
To this communion meal
Remain steadfast with Christ until the end
In all tribulations.

Among the more radical sects of the Reformation were the Anabaptists. They emerged in Zurich and the surrounding area about 1523. Their extreme positions on worship and the sacraments and their absolute pacifism won the enmity of Catholics as well as conservative Protestants such as Martin Luther, John Calvin, and even their spiritual mentor, Huldrych Zwingli.

These verses are excerpts from a hymn of thirty-three stanzas written by George Blaurock (1490-1529). Blaurock had been ordained a Catholic priest, but in 1525 he became the first person to be rebaptized by the Zurich Anabaptists. He was an aggressive evangelist, even interrupting church services to dispute with the preacher. He was arrested in Innsbruck and burned at the stake as a heretic.

Today, Blaurock's hymns are still sung by Amish congregations, the spiritual descendants of the Swiss Anabaptists.

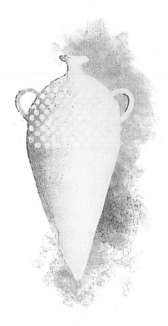

Saint Thomas Aquinas's Prayer after Communion

Most sweet Jesus, may your most sacred body and blood be the delight and pleasure of my soul, salvation and strength in all temptations, joy and peace in all tribulations, light and guide in every word and action, and final protection in death. Amen.

Saint Thomas Aquinas (1225-1274) is generally known as the foremost theologian and Christian philosopher of the Middle Ages. Yet Aquinas was also one of the great contemplatives. His hymns and prayers to Christ present in the Holy Eucharist are among the finest ever written and are still sung in Catholic churches. This brief prayer is one Aquinas composed for his own private use.

Anima Christi

Anima Christi, sanctifica me.
Corpus Christi, salve me.
Sanguis Christi, inebria me.
Aqua lateris Christi, lava me.
Passio Christi, conforta me.
O bone Iesu, exaudi me.
Intra tua vulnera absconde me.
Ne permittas me separari a te.
Ab hoste maligno defende me.
In hora mortis meae voca me.
Et iube me venire ad te,

ut cum Sanctis tuis laudem te
in saecula saeculorum. Amen.

———

Soul of Christ, sanctify me.
Body of Christ, save me.
Blood of Christ, inebriate me.
Water from the side of Christ, wash me.
Passion of Christ, strengthen me.
O good Jesus, hear me.
Within your wounds hide me.
Separated from you let me never be.
From the malignant enemy, defend me.
At the hour of death, call me.
And close to you bid me.
That with your saints I may be
Praising you forever and ever. Amen.

Saint Augustine (354-430 C.E.) is commonly believed to be the author of this prayer, but there is no historical evidence to support the tradition. In fact, no one knows the origins of the "Anima Christi." The earliest text of the prayer dates from about 1360, when it was carved on a palace wall in the Spanish province of Andalusia.

A PRAYER OF SAINT AUGUSTINE

Late have I loved you, O Beauty, so ancient and so new, late have I loved you! And behold, you were within me and I was outside, and there I sought for you, and in my deformity I rushed headlong into the well-formed things that you have made. You were with me, and I was not with you. Those outer beauties held me far from you, yet if they had not been in you, they would not have existed at all. You called, and cried out to me and broke open my deafness; you shone forth upon me and you scattered my blindness: You breathed fragrance, and I drew in my breath and I now pant for you: I tasted, and I hunger and thirst; you touched me, and I burned for your peace.

Saint Augustine was bishop of Hippo in North Africa. After Saint Paul the Apostle, no theologian has had a greater influence on Christianity and on the thought of the West than Augustine. The son of a Christian mother and a pagan father, Augustine spent his young adulthood as a Manichean, a follower of a philosophy that believed in two gods—one good, the other evil—that were in constant conflict with one another. Largely through the influence of Saint Ambrose, bishop of Milan, Augustine was converted to Christianity; he was baptized by Ambrose in 387 C.E. His *Confessions*, from which this prayer comes, is Augustine's dramatic, emotional account of his life, his conversion, and his intellectual and spiritual development.

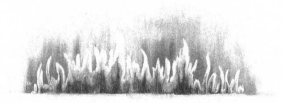

FROM THE SURA OF LIGHT

Allah is the Light of the heavens and the earth. The similitude of His light is as a niche wherein is a lamp. The lamp is in a glass. The glass is as it were a shining star. [The lamp is] kindled from a blessed tree, an olive neither of the East nor of the West, whose oil would almost glow forth [of itself] though no fire touched it. Light upon light, Allah guideth unto His light whom He will. And Allah speaketh to mankind in allegories, for Allah is Knower of all things.

Sura XXIV, 35

This verse lies at the heart of Sura XXIV, a sura dedicated to the Light of Allah, which should shine in the homes of believers. The bulk of the sura details how Muslim families may live pure lives within their homes.

A PRAYER OF SAINT CLARE OF ASSISI

Place your mind before the mirror of eternity!
Place your soul in the brilliance of glory!
Place your heart in the figure of the divine substance!
And transform your whole being into the image of the
Godhead Itself through contemplation!
So that you too may feel what His friends feel
as they taste the hidden sweetness

which God Himself has reserved
from the beginning
for those who love Him.

As Saint Francis's partner in pursuing the ideals of radical poverty and total commitment to Christ, Saint Clare of Assisi (c. 1193-1254) struggled her whole life to win papal approval for her community of cloistered nuns—approval the Pope finally granted as she lay on her deathbed. This ecstatic prayer is found in a letter Clare was writing to Blessed Agnes of Prague, princess of Bohemia, who had founded a convent that was attempting to follow Clare's austere rule.

MYSTICAL POEM OF RUMI (394)

The lord of beauty and quintessence of loveliness entered the soul and mind as a man will stroll in the garden at spring.

Come, come, for you are the life and salvation of men; come, come, for you are the eye and lamp of Joseph.

Lay foot on my water and clay, for through your foot darkness and veiledness depart from water and clay.

Through your glow stones turn to rubies, through your searching the searcher reaches his goal.

Come, come, for you bestow beauty and glory; come, come, for you are the cure of a thousand Jacobs.

Come, come, though you have never departed, but I speak every word to you for a desired end.

Sit in the place of my soul, for you are a thousand times my soul; slay your paramour and lover, for you are the Beloved.

If the king is not the king of the world, O melancholy world, by His life I bid you say, "Why are you in confusion?"

Now you are gay and fresh with His green banner, and now you are overturned by the heat of his army of battle.

Now, like the thought of an artist, you fashion forms; now you sweep carpets like a broom of the porter.

When you sweep a form, you give its quintessence angelhood, and the wings and pinions of the cherubim.

Silence, guard the water strictly like a waterbag, for if you sprinkle it through a crack, know that you are at fault.

Your heart has reached Shams, the Pride of Tabriz, because the Doldol of the heart proved itself a nimble mount.

At the conclusion of this mystical hymn, Jalal al-Din Rumi refers to the wandering dervish, Shams al-Din of Tabriz, who converted Rumi to an ecstatic form of Islam. Doldol was the mule owned by Ali, Muhammad's first convert and his son-in-law.

A Prayer of Saint Catherine of Siena

O immeasurably tender love! Who would not be set afire with such love? What heart could keep from breaking? You, deep well of charity, it seems you are so madly in love with your creatures that you could not live without us! Yet you are our God, and have no need of us. Your greatness is no greater for our well-being, nor are you harmed by any harm that comes to us, for you are supreme eternal Goodness. What could move you to such mercy? Neither duty nor any need you have of us (we are sinful and wicked debtors!)—but only love!

If I see clearly at all, supreme eternal Truth, it is I who am the thief, and you have been executed in my place. For I see the Word, your Son, nailed to a cross. And you have made him a bridge for me, as you have shown me, wretched servant that I am! My heart is breaking and yet cannot break for the hungry longing it has conceived for you!

Christened Caterina di Giacomo di Benincasa, Saint Catherine of Siena (1347-1380) is one of Christianity's greatest mystics. With Saint Teresa of Avila and Saint Thérèse of Lisieux, she is also one of the three women to be proclaimed Doctor of the Church for her sublime works of spirituality. This prayer comes from her most famous mystical work, *The Dialogue*, an ecstatic conversation between Catherine and God the Father.

RABI'A'S PRAYER FOR MYSTICAL UNION

O my God, the best of Thy gifts within my heart is the hope of Thee and the sweetest word upon my tongue is Thy praise, and the hours which I love best are those in which I meet with Thee. O my God, I cannot endure without the remembrance of Thee in this world and how shall I be able to endure without the vision of Thee in the next world? O my Lord, my plaint to Thee is that I am but a stranger in Thy country, and lonely among Thy worshippers.

The theme of the Sufi mystic, Rabi'a, in this yearning prayer is common to mystics in all religious traditions. She compares herself to a lover without her beloved, left alone in a strange place, with only memories of their last meeting for consolation.

Saint Clare of Assisi's Canticle to Poverty

O blessed poverty,
who bestows eternal riches on those who love and embrace her!

O holy poverty,
to those who possess and desire you
God promises the kingdom of heaven
and offers, indeed, eternal glory and blessed life!

O God-centered poverty,
whom the Lord Jesus Christ
Who ruled and now rules heaven and earth,
Who spoke and things were made,
condescended to embrace before all else!

Clare of Assisi was Saint Francis of Assisi's closest colleague. Like him, Clare's commitment to a radical ideal of absolute poverty was unwavering. This canticle in praise of poverty appears in her first letter to Blessed Agnes of Prague, a princess of Bohemia who established a convent in Prague that mirrored Clare's own convent at San Damiano, outside the walls of Assisi.

Mystical Poem of Rumi (251)

Last night I saw Poverty in a dream, I became beside
myself from its beauty.
From the loveliness and perfection of the grace of
poverty I was dumbfounded until dawn.
I saw poverty like a mine of ruby, so that through its
hue I became clothed in silk.
I heard the clamorous rapture of lovers, I heard the
cry of "Drink now, drink!"
I saw a ring all drunken with poverty; I saw its ring in
my own ear.
From the midst of my soul a hundred surgings rose
when I beheld the surging of the sea.
Heaven uttered a hundred thousand cries; I am the
slave of such a leader.

It is undeniable that Rumi and Francis and Clare of Assisi shared a mystical joy
in all creation and in the spiritual delights of poverty. If it is true that Francis
encountered Rumi's mystical poems while he was in Egypt and the Holy Land,
it is also possible that he might have shared what he had learned with Clare, his
closest collaborator. And no work of Rumi would have appealed to Saint Clare
more than this ode to poverty.

Prayers of Contrition and Atonement

Saint Ephraim's Prayer at Midnight

O Lord and Master of my life,
give me not a spirit of sloth,
vain curiosity, lust for power and idle talk.

But give to me, your servant,
a spirit of soberness,
humility, patience and love.

Yea, O Lord and King,
grant me to see my own faults,
and not to condemn my brother;
for blessed are you to the ages of ages. Amen.

Saint Ephraim the Syrian (305-373 C.E.) spent one part of his life as a teacher of theology and another part as an ascetic. His writings are distinctive for their poetic rhythm.

ANSARI'S MUNAJAT (8)

O God, I have neither a key to open a door,
Nor the magnanimity to forgive myself.
O Thou without a partner, divine in the act of creation,
What harm could there be in rescuing an indigent at his last
breath of life?
Without Thy commandment this world would not last a
moment;
Without Thy guidance all creatures would be powerless.
Shouldst Thou overlook all that I have done and not done,
I would gain thereby, and Thou wouldst not lose.

ANSARI'S MUNAJAT (72)

O God, with each day that passes I grow more deficient,
The more I press ahead, the more I fall behind.
O Thou, who hast seen a hundred sins from each breath of mine,
And by Thy grace and charity hast refrained from disclosing them,
Worse am I than any, the worst in the world,
Yet Thy grace has pardoned many worse than I.

Khwajih 'Abd Allah Ansari (1006-1088) was a descendant of Abu Ayyub Khalid ibn Zaid Khazraji, who had sheltered Muhammad in his house when the Messenger fled to Medina. Ansari, who was born in Afghanistan and was the son of a shopkeeper in the bazaar of Herat, acquired an education and became a scholar of the Qur'an and a poet who wrote in Persian and Arabic. He won lasting fame as the author of these *Munajat*, or intimate conversations, still considered among the masterworks of Persian literature. As with mystics in all religious traditions, Ansari took a private, highly personal approach to addressing God. By keeping his prayers brief—some are no more than two or three lines long—he brought special power and immediacy to his mystical conversations.

VIDUI

Ashamnu bagadnu gazalnu dibarnu dofi.
He'evinu vehirshanu zadnu hamasnu
tafalnu shaker. Ya'atznu ra, kizavnu latznu
maradnu ni'atznu sararnu 'avinu
pashanu tzararnu kishinu 'oref. Rashanu
shihatnu ti'avnu ta'inu titanu.

V'al kulam Elo-ah selihot, selah lanu, mehal lanu, kapper lanu.

————

We abuse, we betray, we are cruel.
We destroy, we embitter, we falsify.
We gossip, we hate, we insult.
We jeer, we kill, we lie.
We mock, we neglect, we oppress.
We pervert, we quarrel, we rebel.
We steal, we transgress, we are unkind.
We are violent, we are wicked, we are xenophobic.
We yield to evil, we are zealots for bad causes.

For all these sins, forgiving God, forgive us, pardon us,
grant us atonement.

The Vidui is a general confession of sin recited during the Yom Kippur service. It is not uncommon, however, for Jewish congregations to recite this confession at other times during the year as a devotional practice. Furthermore, there is a long tradition of devout Jews reciting the Vidui on their deathbeds.

A GENERAL CONFESSION

Almighty and most merciful Father; We have erred, and strayed from thy ways like lost sheep. We have followed too much the devices and desires of our own hearts. We have offended against thy holy laws. We have left undone those things we ought to have done; And we have done those things which we ought not to have done; And there is no health in us. But thou, O Lord, have mercy upon us, miserable offenders. Spare thou those, O God, who confess their faults. Restore thou those who are penitent; According to thy promises declared unto mankind In Christ Jesus our Lord. And grant, O most merciful Father, for his sake; That we may hereafter live a godly, righteous, and sober life, To the glory of thy holy Name. Amen.

At the service of Evening Prayer of the Anglican Church, the congregation and the clergy kneel and recite this prayer of penitence. The unusual capitalization comes from a venerable tradition of the Anglican Church that every edition of the *Book of Common Prayer* should imitate the earliest text as it was produced by Thomas Cranmer (1489-1556).

THE ACT OF CONTRITION

O my God, I am heartily sorry for having offended thee; and I detest all my sins because of thy just punishments. But most of all, because they offend thee, my God, who art all good and deserving of all my love. I firmly resolve, with the help of thy grace, to sin no more and to avoid the near occasion of sin.

THE CONFITEOR

Confiteor Deo omnipotenti, beatae Mariae semper virgini, beato Michaeli archangelo, beato Joanni Baptistae, sanctis Apostolis Petro et Paulo, et omnibus Sanctis, quia peccavi nimis cogitatione, verbo, et opere: mea culpa, mea culpa, mea maxima culpa. Ideo precor beatam Mariam semper virginem, beatum Michaelem archangelum, beatum Joannem Baptistam, sanctos Apostolos Petrum et Paulum, et omnes Sanctos, orare pro me ad Dominum Deum nostrum.

———

I confess to Almighty God, to blessed Mary, ever virgin, to blessed Michael the Archangel, to blessed John the Baptist, to the holy apostles, Peter and Paul, and to all the saints, that I have sinned exceedingly in thought, word, and deed: through my fault, through my fault, through my most grievous fault. Therefore I beseech blessed Mary, ever virgin, blessed Michael the Archangel, blessed John the Baptist, the holy apostles, Peter and Paul, and all the saints, to pray to the Lord our God for me.

Roman Catholics recite the Act of Contrition after they have confessed their sins to a priest. Since at least the eighth century, the Confiteor has been recited at the beginning of Mass as a public admission of sinfulness.

The Refutation of Disbelief (Kalimatu Raddil-Kufr)

Allahumma inni a'oozu bika min an ushrika bika shai'an wa ana a'lamu wa astaghfiruka lima la a'alamu innaka anta 'Allam ul-ghuyoobi tubtu 'anhu wa tabarr'atu 'an kulli deenin siwa deen il-Islami wa aslamtu wa aqoolu la ilaha ill-Allahu Muhammad-ur-rahsool-ullah.

————

O God! verily do I seek refuge in Thee from associating any partner with Thee knowingly; I beseech Thy forgiveness for the sins which I am not aware of; verily, Thou art the Best Knower of all secrets. I repent for all the sins and make myself proof against all teachings except the teachings of Islam. I have entered the fold of Islam, and I hereby declare:—There is no god but God and Muhammad is the Messenger of God.

This Islamic declaration begs God's forgiveness for not believing in him correctly. The final line of the prayer declares the fundamental principle of Islam.

A Prayer of Saint Sarrah

O Lord, you who have measured the heights and the earth in the hollow of your hand, and created the six-winged Seraphim to cry out to you with an unceasing voice: "Holy, Holy, Holy, glory to your name." Deliver me from the mouth of the evil one, O Master.

Forget my many evil deeds and through the multitude of your compassions grant me daily forgiveness, for you are blessed unto the ages. Amen.

Although there are a host of legends attached to the life of Saint Sarrah (fourth century C.E.), there is very little historical information about her. We do know that she was one of the relatively small number of Christian women who chose an ascetic life and that she was a native of Libya.

An Akkadian Invocation to an Unnamed God

Who is there who has not sinned against his god,
who has constantly obeyed the commandments?
Every man who lives is sinful.
I, your servant, have committed every kind of sin.
Indeed I served you, but in untruthfulness,
I spoke lies and thought little of my sins,
I spoke unseemly words—you know it all.
I trespassed against the god who made me,

acted abominably, constantly committing sins.
I looked at your possessions,
I lusted after your precious silver.
I raised my hand and defiled what was untouchable,
I went into the temple in a state of uncleanness.

I constantly practiced shameful dishonor against you,
I transgressed your commandments in every way that
displeased you.
In the frenzy of my heart I blasphemed your divinity.
I constantly committed shameful acts, aware and unaware,
acted completely as I pleased, slipped back into wickedness.

Enough, my god! Let your heart be still,
may the goddess, who was angry, be utterly soothed.
Desist from your anger which has risen so high in your heart!
May your [ ] by which I swore be completely reconciled with me.
Though my transgressions are many—free me of my guilt!
Though my misdeeds are seven—let your heart be still!
Though my sins be countless—show mercy and heal [me]!
[My god], I am exhausted, hold my hand [ ].

Fragments of this penitential prayer have been found in Nineveh and Ashur.
The text survives in Sumerian and Akkadian texts and even echoes Hittite
prayers.

PSALM 51

Have mercy upon me, O God, according to thy loving kindness: according unto the multitude of thy tender mercies blot out my transgressions.

Wash me thoroughly from my iniquity, and cleanse me from my sin.

For I acknowledge my transgressions: and my sin is ever before me.

Against thee, thee only, have I sinned, and done this evil in thy sight: that thou mightest be justified when thou speakest, and be clear when thou judgest.

Behold, I was shapen in iniquity; and in sin did my mother conceive me.

Behold, thou desirest truth in the inward parts: and in the hidden part thou shalt make me to know wisdom.

Purge me with hyssop, and I shall be clean: wash me, and I shall be whiter than snow.

Make me to hear joy and gladness; that the bones which thou hast broken may rejoice.

Hide thy face from my sins, and blot out all mine iniquities.

Create in me a clean heart, O God; and renew a right spirit within me.

Cast me not away from thy presence; and take not thy holy spirit from me.

Restore unto me the joy of thy salvation; and uphold me with thy free spirit.

Then will I teach transgressors thy ways; and sinners shall be converted unto thee.

Deliver me from bloodguiltiness, O God, thou God of my
salvation: and my tongue shall sing aloud of thy
righteousness.

O Lord, open thou my lips; and my mouth shall shew forth
thy praise.

For thou desirest not sacrifice; else would I give it: thou
delightest not in burnt offering.

The sacrifices of God are a broken spirit: a broken and a
contrite heart, O God, thou wilt not despise.

Do good in thy pleasure unto Zion: build thou the walls of
Jerusalem.

Then shalt thou be pleased with the sacrifices of
righteousness, with burnt-offering and whole burnt-offering:
then shall they offer bullocks upon thine altar.

David, King of Israel, saw Bathsheba, the wife of Uriah, in her bath and was so over-
whelmed by lust for her that he arranged for Uriah to be placed in the front line of
battle against the Philistines. Uriah was killed, and David took Bathsheba as his wife.
Sometime later, Nathan the prophet confronted David with his sin and announced
that God would punish the king by taking the life of his and Bathsheba's infant son.
Tradition says David composed this psalm in penitence for his crime.

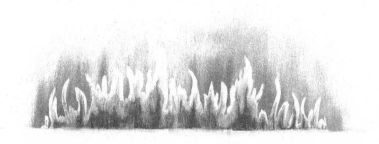

Confession to Tara

I create not just one negative action in a day, but many times in a day, countless negative actions in a week and a month, countless such actions in a year, much more in a lifetime, as well as in all my previous lives. I have created such a limitless number of negativities that, if they had form, they would not fit in the endless sky; and a number of accumulating negativities which is beyond the Buddha's thought, much more so beyond the thought of worldly beings. I am the worst sinner. It seems I would remain in hell forever, even after all attain Buddhahood. I have created for myself such a great loss, if I were to die right at this moment it would be too horrible.

Please, I pray to the Three Jewels, Buddha, Dharma, and Sangha, look upon me with your limitless compassion, and consider upon me. Please forgive me for having created these countless negativities, and help me to completely purify myself. Please eradicate, at this very moment, all the negativities of body, speech, and mind, which have been accumulated from countless lives.

From today on I will never create such karma, it is completely decided.

As Chenresig, the Buddha of Compassion, observed the agonies creatures suffer on earth, he shed a single tear. From that tear was born the goddess Tara, the female embodiment of the highest wisdom and the essence of all Buddhas and Bodhisattvas. In her loving kindness, Tara saves souls from the endless cycle of birth, death, and rebirth. This confession of sin comes from a longer prayer begging Tara for her help to overcome the impulse to indulge in negative actions.

PRAYER BEFORE A CRUCIFIX

Behold, O kind and most sweet Jesus, I cast myself upon my knees in your sight, and with the most fervent desire of my soul I pray and beseech you that you would impress upon my heart lively sentiments of Faith, Hope, and Charity, with true repentance for my sins and a firm desire of amendment, while with deep affection and grief of soul I ponder within myself and mentally contemplate your five most precious wounds; having before my eyes that which David spoke in prophecy of you, O good Jesus: "They have pierced my hands and my feet; they have numbered all my bones."

Among Roman Catholics, this prayer is commonly part of the Stations of the Cross devotion, in which the faithful meditate on fourteen episodes in the suffering and death of Jesus, from his condemnation by Pontius Pilate to his burial. It can be found in most prayer books, always accompanied by a small engraving of Christ on the cross.

A PRAYER OF JOHN CALVIN

Let us fall down before the majesty of our God and acknowledge our offenses, beseeching him to have mercy upon us that we may find favor at his hands, although we deserve it not, and beseeching him to pardon not only the sins which we have already committed but also to rid us of all our faults, until he hath clothed us with the perfection of his holiness, whereunto he daily exhorteth us. Amen.

After fleeing Catholic authorities in France, John Calvin (1509-1564) attempted to establish a perfect Protestant theocracy in Geneva. This prayer reflects his belief that God sends his people difficulties and trials to punish them for their sins and remind them to return to the ways of righteousness. For Calvin, a Christian must never rebel against these sufferings but must submit to them and repent.

A Prayer of John Knox

Omnipotent and everlasting God, Father of our Lord Jesus Christ, who by thy eternal providence disposest kingdoms as seemeth best to thy wisdom: We acknowledge and confess thy judgments to be righteous, in that thou hast taken from us, for our ingratitude, and for the abusing of thy most holy Word, our native king and earthly comforter.

Justly mayest thou pour forth upon us the uttermost of thy plagues, for we have not known the days and time of our merciful visitation. We have scorned thy Word, and despised thy mercies; we have transgressed thy laws, for deceitfully have we wrought, every man with our neighbor; oppression and violence we have not abhorred; charity hath not appeared among us, as our profession requires. We have little regarded the voices of thy prophets. Thy threatenings we have believed to be vanity and wind. So that in us, of ourselves, there remains nothing worthy of thy mercy, for all are found fruitless; even the princes with the prophets, as withered trees apt and meet to be burned in the fire of thy eternal displeasure.

But, O Lord, behold thy own mercy and goodness, that thou mayest purge and remove the burden of our most horrible offenses. Let thy love overcome the severity of thy judgments, even as it did in giving to the world thy only Son, Jesus, when all mankind was lost, and no obedience was left in Adam or in his seed. Regenerate our hearts, O Lord, by the strength of the Holy Spirit. Convert thou us, and we shall be converted. Work thou in us unfeigned repentance, and move thou our hearts to obey thy holy laws. Take not from us the light of thy gospel. Repress thou the pride of those that would rebel; and remove from all hearts the contempt of thy Word. Look thou to the honor of thy own name, O Lord; and let thy gospel be preached with boldness in this realm. If thy justice must punish, then punish our bodies with the rod of thy mercy and let us not faint under the cross of our Savior, but assist us with the Holy Spirit, even to the end.

Of all the early Protestants, the Scottish reformer John Knox (c. 1513-1572) was the most severe. Even today, he is a controversial figure in the history of the Reformation. Knox wrote this prayer in 1553, upon the death of the Protestant King Edward VI of England and the accession of Mary I, his Catholic half-sister, to the throne. For Knox, it seemed the end of Protestantism in England, but like Calvin he interpreted this serious setback as a judgment on Protestant Christians for their sins.

The Prayer of Saint Genesius of Rome

There is no King but him whom I have seen; he it is that I worship and adore. Were I to be killed a thousand times for my allegiance to him, I should still go on as I have begun, I should still be his man. Christ is on my lips, Christ is in my heart; no torments can ever take him from me. I am very sorry for the mistake I made in sneering at the holy name in holy men and coming so late to worship the true King, thinking I knew better than to be a soldier of his.

It is believed (although far from certain) that this extraordinary prayer was recorded by an eyewitness at the martyrdom of Genesius about 285 C.E. Genesius was an actor in Rome, and he is said to have been touched by grace while performing a parody of Christians before the Emperor Diocletian. When Diocletian understood that Genesius's sudden conversion was sincere, he had him tortured to death. Saint Genesius is invoked as the patron of actors.

A Good Resolution

I mean to be obedient,
And cross my ugly nature,
And share the blessings that are sent
To ev'ry honest creature;
With ev'ry gift I will unite
And join in sweet devotion:
To worship God is my delight,
With hands and feet in motion.

In the Shaker communities west of the Alleghenies, few hymn writers were more prolific than Richard McNemar, the author of this march. The final lines of worshiping God "with hands and feet in motion" allude to the ecstatic dancing that was the most characteristic feature of Shaker religious rituals. "A Good Resolution" appears in McNemar's hymnal, *A Selection of Hymns and Poems: For the Use of Believers*, published at the Shaker settlement of Watervliet, Ohio in 1833. It was probably sung to the melody of "Yankee Doodle," a favorite tune of the early Shakers.

KOL NIDRE (ALL VOWS)

Kol nidre weesare waharame,
wekoname, wekinnuye, ukenase,
ushebu'ot dinedarna, udeishteba'na udea harimna,
wediasarna 'al nafshatana miyom kippurim zeh,
'ad yom kippurim habba 'alenu letobah kullehon
iharatna behon,
kullehon yehon sharan,
shebikin, shebitin, betelin, umebuttalin, losheririn,
welo kayyamin;
nidrana lanidre weesarana la esare,
ushebu 'atana lashebu'ot.

———

All vows, obligations, oaths, and anathemas
which we may vow, swear, or pledge, or whereby we
may be bound, from this Yom Kippur until the next
(whose happy coming we await), we do repent.
May they be deemed absolved, forgiven, annulled, and
void, and made of no effect;
they shall not bind us nor have power over us.
The vows shall not be reckoned vows;
the obligations shall not be obligatory;
nor the oaths be oaths.

Yom Kippur, the Day of Atonement when Jews repent for the sins they have committed during the past year, begins at an evening service with the singing of this prayer. The Kol Nidre releases Jews only from vows made to God, not from any vows or oaths made to people.

Prayers of Faith and Trust in God

THE TAWAF

Bismillahi walhamdu lillahi wallahu Akbar wassalatu was-salamu 'ala Rasoolillah.

———

I begin in the name of God, and all Praise is due to God and God is Greater, and peace and blessings be on God's Messenger.

———

Allahummaghfirli zunoobi wa tahhir li qalbi wa ashrah li sadri wa yassir li amri wa 'afini fi man 'afait.

———

O God! forgive me my sins and purify my heart and expand my chest and make my task easy and preserve me among those Thou hast preserved.

———

Allahumma imanam bika wa tasdiqan bikitabika wa wafa'an bi'ahdika wattiba'an li sunnati nabiyyika Muhammadun, sallallahu ta'ala 'alaihi wa sallama, wa ashhadu an la ilaha ill-Allahu wahdahu la sharika lahu wa ashhadu anna Muhammadan 'abduhu wa rasooluhu, amantu billahi wa kafartu bil-jibti wattaghoot.

———

O God! [I am performing this] with complete faith in Thee and belief in the Truth of Thy Book and in the fulfillment of my pledge to Thee, and in the wake of the sunnat of Thy Prophet Muhammad, may peace and blessing of God be upon him. I bear witness to the fact that there is no god but God and that

Muhammad is His Messenger. I have faith in God and do not believe in evil spirits and ghosts.

If circumstances permit, each Muslim should make a pilgrimage to Mecca. The culmination of the pilgrimage ritual is the circumambulation *tawaf*, in which the pilgrim circles the Ka'ba shrine seven times and kisses the Black Stone, all the while offering up these prayers. The "sunnat" of Muhammad are the teachings and the example of the Prophet. The petition to God to "expand my chest" is a metaphor for granting spiritual enlightenment.

A PRAYER OF MARTIN LUTHER

PRAISE TO GOD FOR OVERCOMING EVIL

O Lord, we are not worthy to have a glimpse of heaven, and unable with our works to redeem ourselves from sin, death, the devil, and hell. Nevertheless, thou hast given to us thy Son, Jesus Christ, who is far more precious and dearer than heaven, and much stronger than sin, death, the devil, and hell. For this we rejoice, praise, and thank thee, O God, that without price and out of pure grace thou hast granted us this boundless blessing in thy dear Son through whom thou takest sin, death, and hell from us, and dost grant to us all that belongs to him. Amen.

The preeminent figure of the Protestant Reformation is Martin Luther. In this prayer, Luther emphasizes the primary issue which brought about his split from the Roman Catholic Church: the belief that good works contribute nothing to salvation, which is gained only through unshakable faith in Christ.

An Anabaptist Hymn

God tests as gold
And holds you as his children
If you keep my teachings
I will never leave you.

For I am yours and you are mine
Where I am, there you should be
And who touches you touches my eye
And will be punished on judgment day.

Your misery, fear, anxiety, need and pain
Will then turn to joy
And you will receive praise and honor
Before the hosts of heaven.

The apostles took on such
You should teach it to everyone
Whoever will follow the Lord
Should expect the same.

O Christ, help your people
Who follow you truly
So that through your bitter death
They will be saved from all need.

In the midst of this hymn to Christ, Jesus himself suddenly speaks to comfort and reassure the petitioner that the persecutions the Anabaptists endure are not in vain. He reminds them that the Apostles were also martyred, and the unusual threat that whoever touches them "touches my eye" is an allusion to God's care for Jacob and his children, "He found him in a desert land, and in the waste howling wilderness; he led him about, he instructed him, he kept him as the apple of his eye" (Deuteronomy 32:10).

These verses come from a hymn written by Michael Sattler (1490-1527), a prior of a Benedictine monastery who converted to the Anabaptist cause. An extremely learned man, he presided over the conference of 1527 that defined the Anabaptist faith. A few weeks after the conference ended, Sattler was arrested and condemned. He was tortured on his way to the place of execution, then bound to a ladder and pushed into a fire.

THE LIVING DEAD

Have done with pride and arrogance, conceit, envy, self-assertion;
Practice humility, obedience; worship the Creator.

When a man has abandoned false pride, arrogance, and vainglory,
When he has become humble and meek, then does he find true bliss.

Prince and beggar alike must die: not one survives.
Him do thou call living who has died and yet lives.

My enemy "I" is dead: now none can smite me down.
'Tis I who slay myself: thus, being dead, I live.

We have slain our enemy, we have died; but he is not forgotten.

The thorn remains to vex us. Consider and lay this truth to heart.

Then only wilt thou find the Beloved when thou art as the living dead;
Only by losing thyself canst thou find Him who knoweth all.

Then wilt thou find the Beloved when thou esteemeth thyself as nothing;
Recognize therefore by quiet reflection whence the thought of self arises.

Becoming as the living dead, come thou into the way.
First lay down thy head, then mayest thou venture to plant thy foot.

Know that the way of discipleship is exceeding hard;
The living dead walk in it, the Name of Rama their sign.

So difficult is the way, no living man can tread it;
He only can walk in it, O foolish one, who has died and lives.

Only he who is dead can tread the way that leads to Niranjana;
He finds the Beloved, and leaps the fearsome gulf.

He that is alive shall die: only by dying inwardly shall he meet the Lord;
Forsaking His fellowship who can endure when trouble comes?

O when will this dominion of self pass away? When will the
heart forget every other?
When will it be wholly refined? When will it find its true home?

When I am not, then there is one; when I intrude, then two.
When the curtain of "I" and "you" is drawn aside, then do I
become even as I was.

The sixteenth-century Gujerati mystic Dadu composed this prayer, the creed of
the Dadupanthis sect of Hinduism, which he founded. It is a warning against the
spiritual dangers of pride and an exhortation to "kill" the ego and be reborn as
one in closer communion with Shiva (here referred to as Niranjana).

THE SAINTS' TRIUMPH ON THE DOWNFALL OF ANTICHRIST

Let justice seize old Adam's crew,
And all the whore's production;
We'll take the choicest of their songs,
Which to the Church of God belongs,
And recompense them for their wrongs,
In singing their destruction.

The Shakers knew they were an unconventional sect. While they reveled in their
uniqueness as the only true Christians and were relieved to be separated from the
corruptions of the world, they nonetheless saw no reason not to borrow melodies
from secular songs (such as "Yankee Doodle"!) and the hymns of mainstream
"anti-Christian" churches and set them to new Shaker lyrics. This especially lively example was first printed in 1813 in the *Millennial Praises* hymnal in Hancock,
Massachusetts.

The Prayer of the Infant Jesus

Lo! I am the slave of Allah. He hath given me the Scripture and hath appointed me a Prophet.

And hath made me blessed wheresoever I may be, and hath enjoined upon me prayer and alms-giving so long as I remain alive.

And [hath made me] dutiful toward her that bore me, and hath not made me arrogant, unblest.

Peace on me the day I was born, and the day I die, and the day I shall be raised up alive!

Sura XIX, 30-33

In the sura of Mary (Sura 31) we find a story that follows closely the Annunciation account in the Gospel of Luke. An angel appears to Mary and announces that she will bear a son. Mary protests that she is unmarried and a virgin, but the angel reassures her that by the will of Allah she can conceive a son nonetheless. When Mary returns to her family with her baby in her arms, they refuse to believe that she has been the recipient of a miracle. So the infant Jesus speaks in defense of himself and his mother and to explain his mission.

It is important to remember that in Islam, Jesus is not the Son of God: that Allah is God alone, without any partner, and begets no one is a fundamental principle of the faith. The Jesus of Islam is a prophet and a saint, but he is entirely a man; he has no divine nature.

Prayer at the Great Entrance

Holy, Most High, terrible, Thou Who restest in the holies, O Lord, Thyself sanctify us, and count us worthy of Thy fearful Priesthood, and cause us to approach Thy venerable altar with all good conscience: and purify our hearts from every pollution: chase away from us every evil sensation: hallow our minds and our souls, and grant us to accomplish the worship of our holy fathers with Thy fear, propitiating Thy Face at all times; for Thou art He that blessest and sanctifiest all things, and to Thee we ascribe the glory and the giving of thanks.

Perhaps the most impressive moment in the Divine Liturgy of the Eastern Orthodox Church is the Great Entrance, the procession that carries the bread and wine to the altar. Within a short time, the priest will consecrate these offerings, repeating the words of Christ at the Last Supper, "This is my body . . . this is my blood." When the gifts reach the altar, the priest humbles himself before God and offers this prayer to prepare himself for the great mystery that is about to take place in the sanctuary.

This text comes from the Liturgy of Saint Mark, the rite used by the Coptic Church of Egypt. Saint Mark's is one of Christianity's oldest liturgies, dating at least from the fourth or fifth century.

THE CHERUBICON

Let us, who mystically represent the Cherubim, and sing the thrice-holy hymn to the quickening Trinity, lay by at this time all worldly cares, that we may receive the King of Glory, invisibly attended by the angelic orders. Alleluia.

Let all mortal flesh keep silence, and stand with fear and trembling, and ponder nothing earthly in itself; for the King of Kings, and Lord of Lords, Christ our God, cometh forward to be sacrificed and to be given for food for the faithful; and He is preceded by the choirs of the Angels, with every Domination and Power, the many-eyed Cherubim, and the six-winged Seraphim, that cover their faces and vociferate the hymn, Alleluia, Alleluia, Alleluia.

As the gifts of bread and wine are carried to the altar during the Great Entrance, the choir assumes the role of the angelic choir in Heaven and sings this hymn. It is one of the most sublime moments in the Eastern Orthodox Divine Liturgy. In the Russian Orthodox Church, composers over the centuries have exerted themselves to create the most magnificent music for the Cherubicon.

This text of the great hymn comes from the Liturgy of Saint James. Although tradition attributes it to Saint James, the first bishop of Jerusalem, it is certainly a later rite, dating sometime before 450 C.E.

A PRAYER OF SAINT FRANCIS OF ASSISI

Let the whole of mankind tremble
the whole world shake
and the heavens exult
when Christ, the Son of the living God,
is [present] on the altar
in the hands of a priest.
O admirable heights and sublime lowliness!
O sublime humility!
O humble sublimity!
That the Lord of the universe,
God and the Son of God,
so humbles himself
that for our salvation
He hides himself under the little form of bread!
Look, brothers, at the humility of God
and pour out your hearts before Him!
Humble yourselves, as well,
that you may be exalted by Him.
Therefore,
hold back nothing of yourselves for yourselves
so that
He Who gives Himself totally to you
may receive you totally.

Toward the end of his life, Francis of Assisi (c. 1182-1226) wrote his *Letter to the Entire Order*, encouraging his Franciscan brothers to "show all possible reverence and honor to the most holy Body and Blood of our Lord Jesus Christ" when they offered the Mass. In the midst of the letter, Francis appears to have gone into ecstasy and composed this prayer in honor of the Eucharist.

THE MANIFESTATION OF MITHRAS

Hail, O Lord,
Great Power, Great Might, King, Greatest of gods, Helios, the
Lord of heaven and earth, God of gods:
mighty is your breath;
mighty is your strength, O Lord.
If it be your will,
announce me to the supreme god,
the one who has begotten and made you:
that a man—
I, _____ whose mother is _____, who was born from
the mortal womb of _____ and from the fluid of semen,
and who, since he has been born again from you today, has
become immortal out of so many myriads in this hour
according to the wish of god the exceedingly good—
resolves to worship you,
and prays with all his human power
(that you may take along with you the horoscope of the day
and hour today, which has the name THRAPSIARI MORIROK,
that he may appear and give revelation during the good hours,
EORO RORE ORRI ORIOR ROR ROI OR REORORI EOR EOR EOR
EORE!)

The religion of Mithras in the late Roman Empire blended conventional Greek
and Egyptian religion with magic, elements of the mystery cults, sun worship, and
fire worship. The Mithraic liturgy was a mystical, ecstatic journey of the soul to its
god. This prayer was recited by the faithful to greet the god Mithras when he
appeared to the congregation. The liturgical book from which this prayer is taken
says, "After you have said these things, he will come . . . and you will see him walking. . . . Look intently, and make a long bellowing sound, like a horn, releasing all
your breath and straining your sides." The strange words that conclude the prayer
are probably an approximation of the bellowing that greeted the god.

PRAISE OF RAMA AS THE SUPREME BEING

You are the guardian of the bounds of revelation, O Rama, you are the Lord of the Universe, and Janaki is Maya which creates, preserves and destroys the world at your pleasure, O All Gracious. And Laksmana is the Serpent with a thousand hoods who supports the earth, sovereign of all things animate and inanimate. You have taken a human body for the good of Gods and you have come to destroy the army of demons.

Your real form transcends speech and intelligence. You are ineffable and infinite, called ever by the Vedas: "Not this! not this!" The world is only a drama and you watch it as a spectator, and Brahma, Vishnu, and Shiva you make to dance like puppets. They themselves know not the mystery of your character: who else can then understand you as you are? He alone knows you to whom you have granted the power to know you, and knowing you he becomes one with you.

It is by your Grace, O Raghunandan, that your devotees understand you, you touch the heart of the faithful like refreshing sandalpaste. Your true form is pure thought and bliss, free from change. They know it who have been privileged thus. But for the good of gods and the just, you have taken the form of illusion and you speak and act as a prince of this earth.

O Rama, when they see your actions and when they hear about them, fools are perplexed, but the saints rejoice; whatever you say or do is right.

Tulsidas, a Hindu mystic (died 1623), composed an epic called the *Ramacaritmanas*, the *Sacred Lake of the Acts of Rama*. He was inspired by two classic Sanskrit texts, the Ramayana and the Adhyatma Ramayana. In Tulsidas's work, Rama is the supreme God. Out of compassion for mortals, he takes on human form and comes to earth as a wonder-working hero. Janaki and Laksmana referred to in the prayer are respectively Rama's wife and his brother. The "refreshing sandalpaste" is a fragrant ointment made from powdered sandalwood.

THE PRAISES OF PADMA SAMBHAVA

OM
Stillness and movement have merged
In the womb of the uncreated
I praise you, Great Symbol
All existence has your form
AH

Your stillness utters all sounds
I praise the great Mantra
Which is your voice
HUM

Your emptiness comprehends all thoughts
I praise the Original Mind
Which is your nature

Praise and Blame
Limit the nature of the Universe
Understanding this
I praise you.

Padma Sambhava (eighth century C.E.), also known as the Guru Rinpoche, introduced Tantric Buddhism to Tibet, where he is often visualized as a deity. In

Tibetan Buddhism, the Guru is almost as important as Buddhism's famous Three Jewels—the Buddha, the Dharma, and the Sangha—because the Guru has the power to initiate a disciple into a particular meditation and ensure that the disciple practices it successfully, bringing him or her closer to Enlightenment.

ISAIAH 6:3

IN HEBREW

Kadosh, Kadosh, Kadosh
Adonai tsevaot,
melo chol haarets kevodo.
Baruch kevod Adonai mimekomo.
Ani Adonai Eloheichem!
Yimloch Adonai leolam,
Elohayich Tsiyon,
ledor vador Haleluyah!

———

Holy, holy, holy
is the Lord of Hosts;
the fullness of the whole earth is His glory!
Blessed is the glory of God in heaven and earth.
The Lord shall reign forever;
your God, O Zion, from generation to generation.
Halleluyah!

In Latin

Sanctus, Sanctus, Sanctus,

Dominus Deus Sabaoth.

Pleni sunt coeli et terra gloria tua.

Hosanna in excelsis!

Benedictus qui venit in nomine Domini.

Hosanna in excelsis!

In Greek

Agios, Agios, Agios,

Kyrios Savaoth

pliris o ouranos ke I gi tis doxis Sou.

Osanna en tis Ipsistis!

Evlogimenos o erhomenos en onomati Kyriou.

Osanna en tis Ipsistis!

———

Holy, holy, holy,

Lord God of hosts.

Heaven and earth are filled with your glory.

Hosanna in the highest!

Blessed is he who comes in the name of the Lord.

Hosanna in the highest!

In Isaiah 6:3, the prophet has a vision of the seraphim chanting "Holy, holy, holy" around God's throne. This story has inspired both Jews and Christians of the Western and the Eastern Churches to include the angelic hymn in their liturgies as an expression of the awesome sanctity and ineffable glory of God. In the Jewish Sabbath liturgy, it is said during the Amidah, the prayer that is the focal point of the service. In the Christian liturgy, it is said or chanted before the bread and wine are consecrated, which is the focal point of the communion service. The text is the same in both Latin and Greek, although the Christian version departs somewhat from the Hebrew original.

Prayers of Praise and Awe

Cædmon's Hymn

Nu sculon herigean   heofonrices Weard,
Meotodes meahte   ond his modgethanc,
weorc Wuldorfæder,   swa he wundra gehwæs,
ece Drihten,   or onstealde.
He ærest sceop   eorthan bearnum
heofon to hrofe,   halig Scyppend;
tha middangeard   monncynnes Weard,
ece Drihten,   æfter teode,
firum foldan,   Frea ælmihtig.

Now must we praise the Guardian of the Kingdom of Heaven,
The might of the Creator, and his wisdom,
The work of the Father of Glory; for he, the Eternal Lord,
Appointed each wondrous thing from the beginning.
He, the Holy Creator, first made heaven as a roof for the
children of men;
And afterward he, the Guardian of mankind, the Eternal Lord,
The Almighty Master, fashioned the earth for mortals.

Our only information about Cædmon comes from *A History of the English Church and People*, written by the Venerable Bede (673-755 C.E.). According to Bede, Cædmon was a cowherd at Whitby Abbey in Yorkshire while Saint Hilda was abbess there (657-680 C.E.). During social gatherings in Anglo-Saxon England, it was customary for dinner guests to take turns improvising songs. But Cædmon would always slip away from the feast and hide in the cattle barn because he hadn't the gift for improvisation. One night, a mysterious visitor appeared to Cædmon in the barn and commanded him to "sing the Creation." Miraculously inspired, Cædmon composed this hymn, the oldest surviving Christian prayer composed in English. Cædmon's poem was so esteemed in medieval England that it survives in no less than seventeen manuscripts dating from the eighth through the fifteenth centuries.

The Magnificat (Mary's Canticle)

Magnificat anima mea Dominum:
et exsultavit spiritus meus in Deo salutari meo.
Quia respexit humilitatem ancillae suae:
ecce enim ex hoc beatam me dicent omnes
generationes.
Quia fecit mihi magna qui potens est:
et sanctum nomen eius.
Et misericordia eius a progenie in progenies
timentibus eum.
Fecit potentiam in brachio suo:
dispersit superbos mente cordis sui.
Deposuit potentes de sede,
et exaltavit humiles.
Esurientes implevit bonis:
et divites dimisit inanes.
Suscepit Israel puerum suum,
recordatus misericordiae suae.
Sicut locutus est ad patres nostros,
Abraham et semini eius in saecula.

———

My soul doth magnify the Lord,
And my spirit hath rejoiced in God my savior.
For he hath regarded the low estate of his
handmaiden:
for, behold,
from henceforth
all generations shall call me blessed.
For he that is mighty

hath done to me great things;

and holy is his name.

And his mercy is on them that fear him

from generation to generation.

He hath shewed strength with his arm;

he hath scattered the proud

in the imagination of their hearts.

He hath put down the mighty

from their seats,

and exalted them of low degree.

He hath filled the hungry

with good things;

and the rich he hath sent empty away.

He hath holpen his servant Israel,

in remembrance of his mercy;

As he spake to our fathers,

To Abraham and to his seed forever.

Luke 1:46-55

In the Gospel of Saint Luke, Elizabeth, Mary's elderly cousin who is pregnant with Saint John the Baptist, greets the Blessed Virgin with the words, "Blessed art thou amongst women, and blessed is the fruit of thy womb!" In response, Mary recites this canticle in which she recognizes that the divine plan for human salvation, begun with Abraham, will be brought to fulfillment through her.

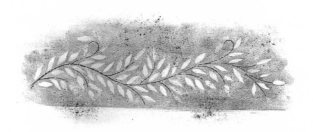

Ar-Rahman	the Beneficent
Ar-Rahim	the Merciful
Al-Malik	the Sovereign Lord
Al-Quddus	the Holy
As-Salam	the Source of Peace
Al-Mu'min	the Guardian of Faith
Al-Muhaymin	the Protector
Al-'Aziz	the Mighty
Al-Jabbar	the Compeller
Al-Mutakabbir	the Majestic
Al-Khaliq	the Creator
Al-Bari'	the Evolver
Al-Musawwir	the Fashioner
Al-Ghaffar	the Forgiver
Al-Qahhar	the Subduer
Al-Wahhab	the Bestower
Ar-Razzaq	the Provider
Al-Fattah	the Opener
Al-'Alim	the All-Knowing
Al-Qabid	the Constrictor
Al-Basit	the Expander
Al-Khafid	the Abaser
Ar-Rafi'	the Exalter
Al-Mu'izz	the Honorer
Al-Muzill	the Dishonorer
As-Sami'	the All-Hearing
Al-Basir	the All-Seeing
Al-Hakam	the Judge
Al-'Adl	the Just

Al-Latif	the Subtle One
Al-Khabir	the Aware
Al-Halim	the Forbearing One
Al-'Azim	the Great One
Al-Ghafur	the All-Forgiving
Ash-Shakur	the Appreciative
Al-'Ali	the Most High
Al-Kabir	the Most Great
Al-Hafiz	the Preserver
Al-Muqit	the Maintainer
Al-Hasib	the Reckoner
Al-Jalil	the Sublime One
Al-Karim	the Generous One
Ar-Raqib	the Watchful
Al-Mujib	the Responsive
Al-Wasi	the All-Embracing
Al-Hakím	the Wise
Al-Wadud	the Loving
Al-Majíd	the Most Glorious One
Al-Ba-'ith	the Resurrector
Ash-Shahid	the Witness
Al-Haqq	the Truth
Al-Wakil	the Trustee
Al-Qawi	the Most Strong
Al-Matin	the Firm One
Al-Wali	the Protecting Friend
Al-Hamid	the Praiseworthy
Al-Muhsi	the Reckoner
Al-Mubdi	the Originator
Al-Mu'id	the Restorer
Al-Muhyi	the Giver of Life
Al-Mumit	the Creator of Death

Al-Hayy	the Alive
Al-Qayyum	the Self-Subsisting
Al-Wajid	the Finder
Al-Májid	the Noble
Al-Wahid	the Unique
Al-Ahad	the One
As-Samad	the Eternal
Al-Qadir	the Able
Al-Muqtadir	the Powerful
Al-Muqaddim	the Expediter
Al-Mu'akhkhir	the Delayer
Al-Awwal	the First
Al-Akhir	the Last
Az-Zahir	the Manifest
Al-Batin	the Hidden
Al-Wali	the Governor
Al-Muta'ali	the Most Exalted
Al-Barr	the Source of All Goodness
At-Tawwab	the Acceptor of Repentance
Al-Muntaqim	the Avenger
Al-'Afuw	the Pardoner
Ar-Ra'uf	the Compassionate
Malik al-Mulk	the Eternal Owner of Sovereignty
Dhul-Jalal-Wal-Ikram	the Lord of Majesty and Bounty
Al-Muqsit	the Equitable
Al-Jame'	the Gatherer
Al-Ghani	the Self-Sufficient
Al-Mughni	the Enricher
Al-Mani'	the Preventer
Ad-Darr	the Distresser
An-Nafi'	the Propitious
An-Nur	the Light

Al-Hadi	the Guide
Al-Badi'	the Incomparable
Al-Baqi	the Everlasting
Al-Warith	the Supreme Inheritor
Ar-Rashid	the Guide to the Right Path
As-Sabur	the Patient

The *subha*, or rosary, is a string of ninety-nine beads plus a large ending bead called a *yad*. The most common *subha* has thirty-three beads and a *yad*, so that a Muslim goes over the beads three times to recite the ninety-nine Beautiful Names of God and the all-inclusive name, Allah, on the *yad*. Tradition asserts that whoever recites the ninety-nine beautiful names will be assured of a place in Paradise. It is not uncommon for devout Muslim women to sing the Beautiful Names of Allah to their children, to impress the essence of the Qur'an upon their hearts while they are still infants.

Another tradition of Islam holds that in fact Allah possesses three thousand names. One thousand are known only to the angels, one thousand are known only to the prophets, three hundred are found in the Jewish Torah, three hundred are found in the Psalms of David, three hundred are found in the Christian New Testament, and ninety-nine are found in the Muslim Qur'an. The final name, the Ism Allah al-a'zam, or the Greatest Name of Allah, is known to Allah alone.

MUSICIAN'S PRAYER TO APOLLO

Phoebus, of you even the swan sings with clear voice to the
beating of his wings, as he alights upon the bank by the
eddying river Peneus; and of you the sweet-tongued minstrel,
holding his high-pitched lyre, always sings both first and last.
     And so hail to you, lord! I seek your favor with my song.

At his birth, Zeus gave Apollo a lyre, and he became god of music and poetry,
presiding over the Muses on Mount Parnassus. This hymn praying for a blessing
on singers was sung in Apollo's temples as part of the liturgy. As with all of the
Homeric hymns, authorship of this prayer is uncertain, but the date is thought to
be between the eighth and sixth centuries B.C.E.

KRISHNA MANIFESTS HIMSELF IN HIS GLORY

Of many mouths and eyes,
Of many wondrous aspects,
Of many marvelous ornaments,
Of marvelous and many uplifted weapons;

Wearing marvelous garlands and garments,
With marvelous perfumes and ointments,
Made up of all wonders, the god,
Infinite, with faces in all directions.

Of a thousand suns in the sky
If suddenly should burst forth
The light, it would be like
Unto the light of that exalted one.

Thou art the Imperishable, the supreme Object of
Knowledge;
Thou art the ultimate resting place of this universe;
Thou art the immortal guardian of the eternal right,
Thou art the everlasting Spirit, I hold.

Without beginning, middle, or end, of infinite power,
Of infinite arms, whose eyes are the moon and sun,
I see Thee, whose face is flaming fire,
Burning this whole universe with Thy radiance.

For this region between heaven and earth
Is pervaded by Thee alone, and all the directions;
Seeing this Thy wondrous, terrible form,
The triple world trembles, O exalted one!

Homage be to Thee from in front and from behind,
Homage be to Thee from all sides, Thou All!
O Thou of infinite might, Thy prowess is unmeasured;
Thou attainest all; therefore Thou art All!

Bhagavad Gita 11:10-12, 15-20, 40

As the warrior Arjuna was preparing to go into battle, he was suddenly filled with horror at the thought of shedding blood. But his chariot driver, Krishna, reassured him and gradually revealed himself to Arjuna as an avatar of Vishnu, the Supreme Lord. This hymn of Arjuna to Krishna is found in the *Bhagavad Gita*, the sacred book that is the cornerstone of the worship of Krishna.

HYMN TO CHRIST THE SAVIOR

You who bridle colts untamed,
who wing unerring birds in flight,
who steer ships along their course
and shepherd the royal lambs,
gather together
your artless children
for honest praising,
guileless hymning
of Christ, the guide of his children.

King of the saints,
invincible Word
of the Father most High,
wisdom's Prince,
Ground of exertion,
eternal Joy;
Jesus, Savior
of this mortal race,
you the Shepherd,
Cultivator,
you the Helmsman
and the Rider,
you the Wing that lifts to heaven
all the company of the saints;
Fisher of men:
them you came to deliver
from the waters of sin;
to fish untainted

by the envious sea
you cast the bait
of sweet fresh life.
Guide your flock
of spiritual sheep;
guide, holy King,
guide your unsullied children.
The prints of Christ's feet
show the way to heaven.

Word everlasting,
Age without end,
undying Light,
Fountain of mercy,
Doer of virtuous deeds,
exalted Life
of them that sing God's praises.

Jesus Christ,
celestial Milk out-pressed
from a young bride's fragrant breasts
(your Wisdom's graces),
your little children
with their tender mouths
slake their thirst there,
drink their fill
of the Spirit flowing
from those incorporeal nipples.

Let us together
sing simple praises,

true hymns
to Christ the King,
our blessed reward
(such is his life-giving teaching).

With hearts undivided
let us sing to the Son in his might.
Votaries of peace,
we the Christ-born,
people of wisdom,
hymn we together
the God of tranquillity.

Saint Clement of Alexandria (died before 215 C.E.) was born to a pagan family and converted to Christianity as a young adult. He received a classical Greek education, and this sublime and sensuous hymn shows the influence of the works of Plato as well as the Bible.

Te Deum

Te Deum laudamus: te Dominum confitemur.
Te aeternum Patrem omnis terra veneratur.
Tibi omnes Angeli; tibi coeli et universae Potestates;
Tibi Cherubim et Seraphim incessabili voce
proclamant:
Sanctus, Sanctus, Sanctus, Dominus Deus Sabaoth.
Pleni sunt coeli et terra maiestatis gloriae tuae.
Te gloriosus Apostolorum chorus,
Te Prophetarum laudabilis numerus,
Te Martyrum candidatus laudat exercitus.
Te per orbem terrarum sancta confitetur Ecclesia,
Patrem immensae maiestatis:
Venerandum tuum verum et unicum Filium;
Sanctum quoque Paraclitum Spiritum.
Tu Rex gloriae, Christe.
Tu Patris sempiternus es Filius.
Tu ad liberandum suscepturus hominem, non
horruisti Virginis uterum.
Tu, devicto mortis aculeo, aperuisti credentibus regna
caelorum.
Tu ad dexteram Dei sedes, in gloria Patris.
Iudex crederis esse venturus.
Te ergo quaesumus, tuis famulis subveni: quos
pretioso sanguine redemisti.
Aeterna fac cum sanctis tuis in gloria numerari.
Salvum fac populum tuum, Domine, et benedic
hereditati tuae.
Et rege eos, et extolle illos usque in aeternum.

Per singulos dies benedicimus te.

Et laudamus nomen tuum in saeculum, et in saeculum saeculi.

Dignare, Domine, die isto sine peccato nos custodire.

Miserere nostri, Domine, miserere nostri.

Fiat misericordia tua, Domine, super nos,

quemadmodum speravimus in te.

In te, Domine, speravi: non confundar in aeternum.

———

We praise thee, O God. We acknowledge thee to be the Lord.

All the earth doth worship thee, O Eternal Father.

To thee all the angels cry aloud, to thee the powers of heaven and of the universe,

To thee the Cherubim and Seraphim in one unceasing voice cry:

Holy, Holy, Holy Lord God of Hosts. Heaven and earth are full of the majesty of thy glory.

The glorious choir of the Apostles praise thee.

The admirable company of the Prophets praise thee.

The white-robed army of Martyrs praise thee.

The holy Church throughout world doth acknowledge thee, the Father of infinite majesty, thy venerable true and only Son, and the Holy Spirit the Comforter.

Thou art the King of glory, O Christ

Thou art the everlasting Son of the Father.

Thou, when thou wouldst take human nature to deliver man, didst not disdain the Virgin's womb.

When thou hadst overcome the sting of death, thou didst open to believers the kingdom of heaven.

Thou sittest at the right hand of God, in the glory of
the Father.

We believe that thou shalt come to be our Judge.

We beseech thee, therefore, help thy servants, whom
thou hast redeemed with thy precious blood.

Make them to be numbered with thy Saints in glory
everlasting.

O Lord, save thy people, and bless thine inheritance.

Govern them and exalt them forever.

Day by day we bless thee; and we praise thy name
forever, yea forever and ever.

Vouchsafe, O Lord, this day to keep us without sin.

Have mercy upon us, O Lord, have mercy upon us.

Let thy mercy be upon us, O Lord, as we have hoped
in thee.

O Lord, in thee have I hoped, let me not be
confounded forever.

The Te Deum, the most majestic of all the ancient prayers of the Church, was
composed about the beginning of the fifth century by an unknown author. Since
the sixth century, the prayer has been sung in convents and monasteries every
Sunday at the end of Matins, except during the penitential seasons of Advent and
Lent. Traditionally, the Te Deum has also been sung at the conclusion of the consecration of churches and the ordination of priests. In the Middle Ages, it was
often the closing hymn of a cycle of mystery plays, and it was common practice
to chant the Te Deum to celebrate a military victory.

HYMN TO PERFECT WISDOM

Homage to Thee, Perfect Wisdom,
Boundless, and transcending thought!
All Thy limbs are without blemish,
Faultless those who Thee discern.

Spotless, unobstructed, silent,
Like the vast expanse of space;
Who in truth does really see Thee
The Tathagata perceives.

As the moonlight does not differ
From the moon, so also Thou
Who aboundest in holy virtues,
And the Teacher of the world.

Those, all pity, who came to Thee,
Buddha-dharmas heralding,
They will win with ease, O Gracious!
Majesty beyond compare.

This excerpt from a long hymn to the Buddha as the personification of Wisdom comes from the Mahayana Buddhist tradition. The Buddha is perfect Wisdom because he has transcended such base impulses as desire and will. For those who have not reached enlightenment, every action they perform is either wholesome or unwholesome. But the Buddha has risen so far above this that his actions are outside the laws of karma.

In Praise of Wisdom

For wisdom is more active than all active things: and
reacheth everywhere by reason of her purity.
For she is a vapor of the power of God, and a certain
pure emanation of the glory of the almighty
God: and therefore no defiled thing cometh
into her.
For she is the brightness of eternal light, and the
unspotted mirror of God's majesty, and the
image of his goodness.
And being but one, she can do all things: and
remaining in herself the same, she reneweth all
things, and through nations conveyeth herself into
holy souls, she maketh the friends of God and
prophets.
For God loveth none but him that dwelleth with
wisdom.
For she is more beautiful than the sun, and above all
the order of the stars: being compared with the
light, she is found before it.
For after this cometh night, but no evil can overcome
wisdom.

Wisdom 7:24-30

In this beautiful passage from the apocryphal Book of Wisdom, the virtue of holy
wisdom is personified as something akin to a breath from God, a sacred and undefiled force that prevails over every evil and inspires holy souls in every generation.

THE DIVINE PRAISES

Blessed be God.

Blessed be his Holy Name.

Blessed be Jesus Christ, true God and true man.

Blessed be the Name of Jesus.

Blessed be his most Sacred Heart.

Blessed be his most Precious Blood.

Blessed be Jesus, the most Holy Sacrament of the altar.

Blessed be the Holy Spirit, the Paraclete.

Blessed be the great Mother of God, Mary most holy.

Blessed be her holy and Immaculate Conception.

Blessed be her glorious Assumption.

Blessed be the name of Mary, virgin and mother.

Blessed be Saint Joseph, her most chaste spouse.

Blessed be God in his angels and in his saints.

This series of exclamations is recited at the Roman Catholic service commonly called Benediction during which the Host, the consecrated Communion bread, is enshrined on an altar for public veneration. The Divine Praises originated in Rome where Father Aloysius Felici, S.J., published them in 1797 to combat blasphemy.

Rites of Passage

Baruch atah Adonai Eloheinu melek ha olam, asher kid'shanu b'mitzvosav, v'tzivanu l'hakhniso bivree so shel Avraham avinu.

———

Blessed art Thou, O Lord our God, King of the universe, who hast sanctified us by Thy commandments, and hast commanded us to enter our son into the covenant of Abraham our father.

K'shem shnikhnas labris kein yikonais l'torah l'huppah ulma'assim tovim.

———

Even as he is entered into the covenant, so may he be led to the Law, the nuptial canopy, and good deeds.

On the eighth day after a Jewish boy is born, his family and friends gather to celebrate the *bris*, the ritual circumcision. The origin of the *bris* goes back to Abraham, the father of the Jewish people. In Genesis 17:9-11, God made a covenant to bless and cherish Abraham's descendants. In return, Abraham swore that he and his descendants would bow to the will of God. The sign of the covenant is circumcision.

After the mohel (the rabbi performing the *bris*) has completed the circumcision, the father recites the benediction given here, and the assembled family, friends and guests respond with the second prayer.

A Mother's Prayer at a Bris Milah

Blessed art Thou, O Lord our God, King of the universe, who hast blessed our union with Thy great gift of life. I thank Thee, O Lord our God, for leading me through anxiety and fear and bestowing this light to replace the uncertainty. Thy great power was with me and my spirit was uplifted and exalted in Thy creation. Thy miracle of love is in the mystery of life coming into being. We thank Thee for the miracle of human experience in the birth of our child. Mayest Thou grant us—mother, father, and child—strength in mind and spirit to raise this infant that he may become the pride and joy of our hearts and be of great honor to God and man.

This contemporary prayer is not a formal part of the *Bris Milah*. Nonetheless, it follows traditional patterns of Jewish prayer and expresses the themes of the ritual.

Naming a Newborn Daughter

Baruch atah Adonai Eloheinu melek ha olam asher nasan lanu toras emes vehayey olam nata besokheynu. Baruch atah Adonai nosein hatorah.

———

Blessed art Thou, O Lord our God, King of the universe, who hast given us the Torah of truth, and hast planted everlasting life in our midst. Blessed art Thou, O Lord, who givest the Torah.

The ritual for naming a Jewish girl takes place during a synagogue service. Customs vary from congregation to congregation. In some congregations, the baby girl is brought to the synagogue to be blessed by the rabbi. Many Reform congregations delay the naming ceremony until the mother and father can come to the temple together with their new daughter.

In traditional congregations, after the Torah has been read, the blessing given above is recited. Then, if a child is to be named that day, the little girl's Hebrew name is announced by the rabbi or the cantor.

Birth Baptism

The little drop of the Father
On thy little forehead, beloved one.

The little drop of the Son
On thy little forehead, beloved one.

The little drop of the Spirit
On thy little forehead, beloved one.

To aid thee from the fays,
To guard thee from the host;

To aid thee from the gnome,
To shield thee from the specter;

To keep thee for the Three,
To shield thee, to surround thee;

To save thee for the Three,
To fill thee with the graces;

The little drop of the Three
To lave thee with the graces.

Alexander Carmichael recorded this chant on the island of Barra in the Outer Hebrides. Many of the outlying islands of Scotland had no priest in residence, so it became the custom for the midwives and nurses to perform a "birth baptism" on newborns until a priest came.

AT HOLY BAPTISM

O merciful God, grant that as Christ died and rose again, so this Child may die to sin and rise to newness of life. Amen.

Grant that all sinful affections may die in him, and that all things belonging to the Spirit may live and grow in him. Amen.

Grant that he may have power and strength to have victory, and to triumph, against the devil, the world, and the flesh. Amen.

Grant that whosoever is here dedicated to thee by our office and ministry, may also be endued with heavenly virtues, and everlastingly rewarded, through thy mercy, O blessed Lord God, who dost live, and govern all things, world without end. Amen.

PRAYER FOR A CHILD'S BIRTHDAY

Watch over thy child, O Lord, as his days increase; bless and guide him wherever he may be, keeping him unspotted from the world. Strengthen him when he stands; comfort him when he is discouraged or sorrowful; raise him up if he fall; and in his heart may thy peace which passeth all understanding abide all the days of his life; through Jesus Christ our Lord. Amen.

In the Anglican service of baptism, after the godparents have renounced Satan and confessed the basic elements of the Christian faith on behalf of the child, the minister offers the first prayer. The second prayer, offered on a child's birthday, is also from the *Book of Common Prayer*.

LITANY FOR THE INITIATION CEREMONY

Leader:	*Group Response:*
The Gazelles. I say the Gazelles. There are Gazelles.	There are!
These people, the Gazelles, which are here, they have become big.	They have become big!
The Mountains also. There are Mountains. There are!	There are!
The Karimojong also, they are.	They are!
There are Karimojong.	There are!
Cattle as well. The cattle of the Mountains. They are.	They are!
The cattle, the cattle of the Mountains, they become fat.	They are fat!
They become fat. Do they not become fat?	They are fat!
The land. This land here. Does it not become good?	It is good!
In this country there are Gazelles.	There are!
The Mountains also, they are.	They are!
Ngipian also. They are here, are they not?	They are!
In this land here, they are.	They are!
There is well-being in our country, is there not?	There is!
It is here.	It is!
Yes. Evil is going away.	It has gone!
It is leaving.	It has gone!
Well-being is with us.	It is!
It will always be with us, will it not?	It will!

It will.	It will!
Will it not?	It will!
God has heard.	He has heard!
He has heard.	He has heard!
The sky. The cloud-spotted sky is here, it has heard.	It has heard.

In the Ngipian region of Uganda, the Karimojong people set up a round enclosure in which young boys (the Gazelles) are initiated into adulthood by older men (the Mountains). While the initiation ceremony is taking place, the other villagers stand outside the enclosure singing this litany. After the rites are completed, the Gazelles roast cattle and serve the meat to the Mountains.

AT THE FIRST MENSTRUATION CEREMONY

Nyankonpon Tweaduapon Nyame [Supreme Sky God, who alone is great], upon whom men lean and do not fall, receive this wine and drink.
Earth Goddess, whose day of worship is a Thursday, receive this wine and drink.
Spirit of our ancestors, receive this wine and drink.
This girl child whom God has given to me, today the Bara state has come upon her.
O mother who dwells in the land of ghosts, do not come and take her away, and do not have permitted her to menstruate only to die.

Among the Ashanti of Ghana, menstruation is a girl's first step toward adulthood, a life journey that reaches completion when she gives birth to her first child. When an Ashanti girl has her first period, her mother takes wine and pours a libation to God and the ancestors, begging them to permit her daughter to live to adulthood and be the mother of children.

GIVING THE WEDDING RING

Harei at mekudeshet li betaba'at zo kedat Moshe v' yisra'el.

———

Thou art consecrated unto me with this ring as my wife,
according to the law of Moses and Israel.

In ancient times, a Jewish couple were betrothed in a formal ceremony a year
before the actual marriage took place (although the betrothal itself was considered as binding as a wedding). By the Middle Ages, the custom of a long
betrothal had disappeared and the wedding ceremony began to combine the
betrothal (*eirusin*) and the marriage rite (*nisu'in*).

After the rabbi has pronounced the Betrothal Blessing, the groom places
the ring on the bride's finger and recites the consecration given above.

THE INVOCATION OF THE GRACES

I bathe thy palms
In showers of wine,
In the lustral fire,
In the seven elements,
In the juice of the rasps [raspberries],
In the milk of honey,
And I place the nine pure choice graces
In thy fair fond face,
The grace of form,
The grace of voice,
The grace of fortune,
The grace of goodness,
The grace of wisdom,

The grace of charity,

The grace of choice maidenliness,

The grace of whole-souled loveliness,

The grace of goodly speech.

Dark is yonder town,

Dark are those therein,

Thou art the brown swan,

Going in among them.

Their hearts are under thy control,

Their tongues are beneath thy sole,

Nor will they ever utter a word

To give thee offense.

This excerpt is taken from a lengthy incantation recited over a bride before she goes to her husband's people. The reference to the bride as a "brown swan" implies that she is very young and not matured into a white swan. Alexander Carmichael said the text came from a woman named Catherine Macaulay from South Uist in the Outer Hebrides.

BLESSING OF A WEDDING RING

Bless (make the Sign of the Cross) thou, O Lord, this ring which we bless (make the Sign of the Cross) in thy name, that he/she who is to wear it may render to his wife/her husband unbroken fidelity. Let him/her abide in thy peace, and be obedient to thy will, and may they live together in constant mutual love. Through Christ our Lord. Amen.

In the Roman Catholic marriage rite, before the groom and the bride place the rings on each other's fingers, the priest makes the Sign of the Cross over the wedding rings and sprinkles them with holy water.

From the Hindu Marriage Rite

Husband:
This am I, that are thou; that are thou, this am I; the heaven I, the earth thou. Come! Let us here marry. Let us beget offspring. Loving, bright, with genial mind may we live a hundred autumns.

Tread on this stone; like a stone be firm. Overcome the enemies; tread the foes down.

So be thou devoted to me. Let us acquire many sons who may reach old age.

Wife:
May my husband live and I get offspring!

A collection of sacred texts called Grhya Sutras details the domestic rituals of Hindu believers. Many of these rites are still practiced, including the marriage rite from which these prayers are taken. All of the prayers are accompanied by ritual gestures such as circling a fire and a water pot, sacrificing melted butter, and pouring grain over the bride's hands to ensure fertility, happiness in the home, and the blessing of the gods.

Petitions from the Sacrament of Marriage

An Angel of Peace, a faithful Guide, a Guardian of our
souls and bodies; let us ask of the Lord.
Pardon and remission of our sins and offenses; let us
ask of the Lord.
All things that are good and profitable for our souls, and
peace for the whole world; let us ask of the Lord.
That we may complete the remaining time of our life
in peace and repentance; let us ask of the Lord.
A Christian ending to our life, painless, without shame,
peaceful; and a good defense before the dread
Judgment Seat of Christ; let us ask of the Lord.
Asking for the unity of the Faith and the Communion
of the Holy Spirit, let us commend ourselves and one
another and all our life to Christ our God.

In the marriage service of the Eastern Orthodox Church, the priest offers each
of these petitions on behalf of the bride and groom and all the assembled congregation, while the choir responds to each, "O Lord, grant this prayer."

PRAYER FOR WEDDED BLISS

Embark the ship of Fortune,
that is whole and unbreakable,
and sailing in that approach the lover
who is according to thy liking.

Call the lover, Lord of wealth!
and make him well inclined in mind;
have him fully on thy right hand,
the lover according to her choice.

This is gold, and this bdellium,
this unguent and this bliss;
May these bring thee to the suitors,
to find one worthy of thy choice.

Atharva-Veda II, 36

THE HOUSEHOLDER'S LIFE

Live you two here, be not parted,
enjoy the full length of life,
sporting with your sons and grandsons,
rejoicing in your own abode.

Rig-Veda X, 85, 42

The first prayer is from a longer hymn for a bride and includes a charm—the gold, bdellium (a fragrant resin like myrrh), and unguent—that will ensure happiness in marriage. The second prayer is one of a series of Hindu blessings called the Asrama for various stages of life.

Death at Hand

Consider this, my Soul, that thou hast none whom thou mayest call thine own. Vain are thy wanderings on the earth. Two days or three, then ends this earthly life; yet all men boast that they are masters here. Time's master, Death, will come and overthrow such masterships. Thy best-beloved, for whom thou art so terribly concerned, will she go with thee? Nay; rather, lest some ill befall the home, she will sprinkle with cow dung the house where thou hast died.

Ramaprasad Sen (1718-1775) was a Bengali mystical poet. This meditation is a classic *memento mori*. It ridicules the delusion that humans exercise any real, enduring mastery in this world. And it shows a lover, rather than longing to join her beloved in death, exorcising his spirit from the house with cow dung so death will not come again.

Prayer of Saint Macrina on Her Deathbed

Lord, you have taken the fear of death away from us. The end of our life here you have made the beginning of true life. For a little while you will let our bodies rest in sleep, and then with the last trumpet you will wake them from their sleep.

You give to the earth to keep for you this earth of ours, which you shaped with your own hands; and you will take it back again, and from a mortal, formless lump transform it into a thing of immortal beauty.

To free us from sin and from the curse laid upon us, you took both sin and the curse upon yourself.

You crushed the head of the dragon that had seized men by the throat and thrust them into the gulf prepared for the disobedient.

When you shattered the gates of hell and trampled the Devil, death's lord, beneath your feet, you cleared the way for our resurrection.

To us who fear you, you gave a sign, the sign of your holy cross, to destroy the Enemy and infuse new vigor into our lives.

O eternal God, you have been my refuge since I left my mother's womb; I love you with all my inmost strength; I have devoted myself body and soul to you from my childhood onwards.

Set now an angel of light beside me and bid him take my hand and lead me to the resting-place where there is water for refreshment, beside the dwellings of the holy fathers.

The flaming sword you snapped in two; the man who hung upon the cross with you and implored your great mercy you restored to paradise. Remember me too, now that you are back in your kingdom, since I also have hung upon the cross with you and the nails have pierced my flesh; for I have always feared your judgment. May the dread gulf not divide me from your elect or the Slanderer stand in my way; may your eyes not rest on my sins.

If out of the weakness of human nature I have fallen and sinned in word or deed or thought, forgive it me; for you have power to forgive sins on earth. When I am divested of my body, may I stand before you with my soul unspotted; receive it, blameless and faultless, with your own hands.

One of the most brilliant and most pious women of the late classical world, Saint Macrina (326-380 C.E.) educated her younger brothers Saint Basil the Great and Saint Gregory of Nyssa in both the fundamentals of the Christian faith and classical Greek culture. The prayer she composed as she was dying was recorded by Gregory, who was at her bedside in her convent in Cappadocia, in what is now Turkey.

LET US WEEP SOFTLY

You, my forefathers, you have congregated here today. Do you not see this? You have taken him with you. I am alone now. . . . I implore you, who are so far, since he has gone back to you, let us remain in peace. He has not left us with that. Let us weep softly over him, in peace. Let us help each other in our pain, even his wife's parents.

In this prayer from South Africa, fear prevents the grieving survivors from offering anything more than a polite rebuke to their ancestors for taking a man's life.

Unction Prayer

Death with unction and with penitence,
Death with joy and with forgiveness,
Death without horror or repulsion,
Death without fear or shrinking.

Dying the death of the saints,
The Healer of my soul by my side,
The death of peace and tranquility,
And grant Thou me a good day of burial.

The seven angels of the Holy Spirit
And two attendant angels
be shielding me, and be this night the night
Till brightness and summer-tide shall come!

The Roman Catholics Alexander Carmichael met in the Highlands and Scottish islands hoped for a "happy death," by which they meant the chance to confess their sins to a priest, to be anointed with holy oil, to receive Holy Communion for the last time, and to have a death hymn such as this one sung over them.

THE FUNERAL HYMN

Slide down to Earth, thy mother; to this Earth
which is wide-spreading and benevolent.
May she, youthful, wool-soft to the devout,
protect thee from annihilation's lap.

Rise up above him, Earth, do not press him down;
be easy of access to him, tend him gently;
cover him up as a mother
wraps her child with the end of her robe.

May Earth rising above him lie lightly,
may a thousand clods cling close together above him,
may these make a home yielding him comfort,
let there be a refuge for him here for ever.

For thee I heap up this earth—heap it around thee.
In placing this clod of earth may I not be harmed.
May the Fathers sustain this thy monument,
may Yama erect a mansion for thee here.

Rig-Veda X, 18

At the time when the Vedas were written, Hindus practiced burial, and today when a yogi dies he is buried rather than cremated. These stanzas, excerpted from a longer funeral hymn, convey themes that recur in many religious traditions: the peace of the grave, the faith in an afterlife, the hope that the King of Heaven (Yama) will guard the place of burial and have a mansion ready for the departed soul.

Man, that is born of a woman, hath but a short time to live, and is full of misery. He cometh up, and is cut down, like a flower; he fleeth as it were a shadow, and never continueth in one stay.

In the midst of life we are in death; of whom may we seek for succor, but of thee, O Lord, who for our sins art justly displeased?

Yet, O Lord God most holy, O Lord most mighty, O holy and most merciful Savior, deliver us not into the bitter pains of eternal death.

Thou knowest, Lord, the secrets of our hearts; shut not thy merciful ears to our prayer; but spare us, Lord most holy, O God most mighty, O holy and merciful Savior, thou most worthy Judge eternal, suffer us not, at our last hour, for any pains of death, to fall from thee.

The *Book of Common Prayer* of the Anglican Church is largely the work of Henry VIII's Archbishop of Canterbury, Thomas Cranmer. Many of the book's prayers have long been admired as masterworks of English prose, and perhaps the finest among them is this sublime prayer from the burial service.

THE SOUL'S PRAYER

O my father Osiris, thou hast done for me that which thy father Ra did for thee. Let me abide upon the earth permanently. Let me keep possession of my throne. Let my heir be strong. Let my tomb, and my friends who are upon the earth, flourish. Let my enemies be given over to destruction, and to the shackles of the goddess Serq. I am thy son. Ra is my father. On me likewise thou hast conferred life, strength, and health. Horus is established upon this tomb. Grant thou that the days of my life may come unto worship and honor.

From certain characteristics of the papyrus, Ani's *Book of the Dead* is thought to date from 1450-1400 B.C.E. But it is not known under which pharaoh the scribe Ani served. The prayers, incantations, charms, and hymns of the *Book of the Dead* go back at least six thousand years and were composed to ensure the immortality of the deceased. This prayer of the soul comes from "The Chapter of Not Dying a Second Time," when the soul prays to Osiris, Lord of the Underworld, to grant him eternal life, just as Ra the Sun God resurrected the dead Osiris and gave him immortality. At the end of the prayer, the soul identifies itself with Horus, the son of Osiris.

THE DEATH OF THE RIGHTEOUS

But the souls of the just are in the hand of God, and the torment of death shall not touch them.

In the sight of the unwise they seemed to die: and their departure was taken for misery:

And their going away from us, for utter destruction: but they are in peace.

And though in the sight of men they suffered torments, their hope is full of immortality.

Afflicted in few things, in many they shall be well rewarded: because God hath tried them, and found them worthy of himself.

As gold in the furnace he hath proved them, and as a victim of a holocaust he hath received them, and in time there shall be respect had to them.

The just shall shine, and shall run to and fro like sparks among the reeds.

They shall judge nations, and rule over people, and their Lord shall reign forever.

They that trust in him, shall understand the truth: and they that are faithful in love shall rest in him: for grace and peace is to his elect.

Wisdom 3:1-9

The Book of Wisdom, part of the Apocrypha, is included in the canon of the Bible by Catholic and Eastern Orthodox Christians, but is rejected by Protestants. The book dates from 100 B.C.E. and, according to the most reliable scholarship, appears to have been written by a Jew of Alexandria, Egypt, who was very well acquainted with the Hebrew Bible. In Christian churches, this passage has traditionally been applied to the sufferings of the martyrs, but it is also a favorite in liturgies for the dead.

For the Comfort of Christ's Presence

O Lord Jesus Christ, who Thyself didst weep beside the grave, and art touched with the feeling of our sorrows; Fulfill now Thy promise that Thou wilt not leave Thy people comfortless, but wilt come to them. Reveal Thyself unto Thine afflicted servants, and cause them to hear Thee saying, "I am the Resurrection and the Life." Help them, O Lord, to turn to Thee with true discernment, and to abide in Thee through living faith, that finding now the comfort of Thy presence, they may have also a sure confidence in Thee for all that is to come: until the day break, and these shadows flee away. Hear us for Thy great mercy's sake, O Jesus Christ our Lord. Amen.

This prayer, which appears in the Presbyterian burial service, begins with an allusion to Christ weeping beside the tomb of his friend Lazarus (John 11:33-38) whom he raised from the dead. Although it is a formal, approved text, this prayer, like every other one in the *Book of Common Worship*, is given under the rubric "for Voluntary Use." This is a reminder of an essential tenet of Presbyterianism: every congregation is free to worship as it sees fit, and none may be compelled to follow any formal ritual.

He is God; what he does is right, for all his ways are just; God of faithfulness and without wrong, just and right is he.

He is God, perfect in every deed; who can say to him: "What art thou doing?" He rules below and above; he causes death and life; he brings down to the grave and raises up.

He is God, perfect in every deed; who can say to him: "What art thou doing?" O thou who decreest and performest, show us unmerited kindness; for the sake of Isaac who was bound like a lamb, listen and take action.

O thou who art righteous in all thy ways, thou who art the perfect God, slow to anger and full of mercy, have compassion, have pity on parents and children; for thine, O Lord, is forgiveness and mercy.

Just art thou, O Lord, in causing death and life; thou in whose hands all living beings are kept, far be it from thee to blot out our remembrance; let thy eyes be open to us in mercy; for thine, O Lord, is mercy and forgiveness.

Whether one lives a year or a thousand years—what does he gain? He is as though he were non-existent. Blessed be the true Judge who causes death and life.

Blessed be he, for his judgment is true; his eye ranges over all, and he punishes and rewards man according to strict account; all must render acknowledgment to him.

We know, O Lord, that thy judgment is just; thou art right when thou speakest, and justified when thou givest sentence; one must not find fault with thy manner of judging. Thou art righteous, O Lord, and thy judgment is right.

True and righteous Judge, blessed art thou, all whose judgments are righteous and true.

The life of every living being is in thy hand; thy right hand is full of righteousness. Have mercy on the remnant of thy own flock, and say to the angel: "Stay your hand."

Thou art great in counsel and mighty in action; thine eyes are open to all the ways of men, to give to every one according to his conduct and according to the results of his doings.

We proclaim that the Lord is just. He is my stronghold, and there is no wrong in him.

The Lord gave and the Lord has taken away; blessed be the name of the Lord.

He is merciful, forgives iniquity and does not destroy; frequently he turns his anger away, and does not stir up all his wrath.

Rabbi Hanina ben Teradyon and his family are said to have recited the opening lines of what has become the Jewish burial service as they were martyred by the Romans, about 135 C.E.

Mourners' Kaddish

Yisgaddal v'yiskaddash shmey rabboh
B'olmoh dee v'roh chir-usey
V'yamlich malchusey
B'cha-yeychon uvyo-meychon
Uvcha-yey d'chol beys yisro-eyl
Ba-agoloh uvizman koreev
V'imru omeyn.

Y'hey shmey rabboh m'vorach
L'olam ul'olmey olmayoh.

Yisborach v'yishtabbach
V'yispo-ar v'yisromam
V'yisnassey v'yis-haddar
V'yis-alleh v'yis-hallal
Shmey d'kudshoh b'reech hu
L'eyloh min kol birchosoh v'shirosoh
Tush-b'chosoh v'nechemosoh
Da-amiron b'olmo
V'imru omeyn.

Y'hey shlomoh rabboh min sh'mah-yoh
V'cha-yeem, oleynu v'al kol yisro-eyl
V'imru omeyn.
O-seh sholom bimromov
Hu ya-aseh sholom
Oleynu v'al kol yisro-eyl
V'imru omeyn.

Glorified and sanctified be God's great name throughout the world which he has created according to his will. May he establish his kingdom in your lifetime and during your days, and within the life of the entire house of Israel, speedily and soon; and say, Amen.

May his great name be blessed forever and to all eternity.

Blessed and praised, glorified and exalted, extolled and honored, adored and lauded be the name of the Holy One, blessed be he, beyond all the blessings and hymns, praises and consolations that are ever spoken in the world; and say, Amen.

May there be abundant peace from heaven, and life, for us and for all Israel; and say, Amen.

As he has brought peace to heaven, so may he bring peace to us and to Israel; and say, Amen.

The Mourners' Kaddish is an Aramaic prayer and is more than two thousand years old. The custom of reciting it for the dead dates from the Middle Ages. The precise reason why this prayer was chosen to remember the dead is uncertain—perhaps because it waits for the future day when God will redeem the entire world. The strictest interpretation of Jewish law requires that the Kaddish cannot be recited unless ten adult Jewish men are present: to mourn a parent, the Kaddish should be recited three times a day for eleven months. The prayer is also recited by family members on the annual anniversary of a death.

Prayers for the Dead

Requiem Eternam

Requiem eternam dona eis Domine, et lux perpetua luceat eis.
Animae eorum et animae omnium fidelium defunctorum per
misericordiam Dei requiescant in pace. Amen.

———

Eternal rest grant unto them, O Lord, and let perpetual light
shine upon them. May their souls, and all the souls of the faithful
departed, through the mercy of God, rest in peace. Amen.

In Paradisum

In paradisum deducant te angeli. In tuo adventu suscipiant te
martyres, et perducant te in civitatem sanctam Ierusalem.
Chorus angelorum te suscipiat. Et cum Lazaro quondam
paupere eternam habeas requiem.

———

May the angels lead you to Paradise. May the martyrs receive
you at your coming and conduct you to the Holy City,
Jerusalem. May choirs of angels receive you. And with Lazarus,
who once was poor, may you have eternal rest.

Subvenite

Subvenite sancti Dei, occurrite angeli Domini. Suscipientes
animam eius, offerentes eam in conspectu Altissimi. Suscipiat
te Christus, qui vocavit te, et in simum Abrahae angeli

deducant te. Suscipientes animam eius, offerentes eam in conspectu Altissimi.

———

Come to his assistance, you Saints of God. Come forth to meet him, you angels of the Lord. Receive his soul and offer it in the sight of the Most High. May Christ who has called you receive you, and may the angels lead you into Abraham's bosom. Receive his soul and offer it in the sight of the Most High.

PSALM 130, DE PROFUNDIS

De profundis clamavi ad te, Domine:
Domine, exaudi vocem meam:
Fiant aures tuae intendentes,
in vocem deprecationis meae.
Si iniquitates observaveris, Domine:
Domine, quis sustinebit?
Quia apud te propitiatio est:
et propter legem tuam sustinui te, Domine.
Sustinuit anima mea in verbo eius:
speravit anima mea in Domino.
A custodia matutina usque ad noctem:
speret Israel in Domino.
Quia apud Dominum misericordia:
et copiosa apud eum redemptio.
Et ipse redimet Israel,
ex omnibus iniquitatibus eius.

———

Out of the depths
have I cried unto Thee, O Lord.

Lord, hear my voice:
let thine ears be attentive
to the voice of my supplications.
If thou, Lord, shouldest mark iniquities,
O Lord, who shall stand?
But there is forgiveness with thee,
that thou mayest be feared.
I wait for the Lord,
my soul doth wait,
and in his word do I hope.
My soul waiteth for the Lord
more than they that watch for the morning:
I say, more than they that watch for the morning.
Let Israel hope in the Lord:
for with the Lord there is mercy,
and with him is plenteous redemption.
And he shall redeem Israel
from all his iniquities.

These prayers, which are commonly recited by Catholics when they pray for the dead, are also part of the Mass and Office for the Dead. They date at least from the tenth century. Psalm 130, of course, is much more ancient—about three thousand years old.

THE INVOCATION OF THE BUDDHAS AND BODHISATTVAS

O ye Compassionate Ones, defend [name of the deceased] who is defenseless. Protect him who is unprotected. Be his forces and his kinsmen. Protect [him] from the great gloom of the Bardo. Turn him from the red [storm] wind of Karma. Turn him from the great awe and terror of the Lords of Death. Save him from the long narrow passage-way of the Bardo.

O ye Compassionate Ones, let not the force of your compassion be weak; but aid him. Let him not go into misery. Forget not your ancient vows; and let not the force of your compassion be weak.

O ye Buddhas and Bodhisattvas, let not the might of the method of your compassion be weak towards this one. Catch hold of him with [the hook of] your grace. Let not the sentient being fall under the power of evil karma.

In Tibetan Buddhism, the only terror death holds for believers is that they will be trapped in the Bardo, the intermediate state between death and rebirth, rather than achieving Nirvana, which is the final liberation from the cycle of birth, death, and rebirth. To hasten the departed toward final liberation, the living call upon the help of the Buddhas and Bodhisattvas, the thousands of compassionate incarnations of the Buddha.

With the souls of the righteous dead, give rest, O Savior, to the soul of thy servant, preserving him unto the life of blessedness which is with thee, O Thou who lovest mankind.

In the place of thy rest, O Lord, where all thy Saints repose, give rest also to the soul of thy servant, for thou alone lovest mankind.

Glory be to the Father and to the Son, and to the Holy Spirit.

Thou art the God who didst descend into hell and loose the bonds of the captives. Do thou give rest also to the soul of thy servant.

Both now and forever and unto the ages of ages.

O Virgin, alone pure and undefiled, who without seed didst bring forth God, pray thou that his soul may be saved.

With the Saints give rest, O Christ, to the soul of thy servant, where there is neither sickness, nor sorrow, nor sighing, but life everlasting.

What earthly pleasure remains unmixed with grief? What glory stands unshaken on earth? All things are flimsier than shadows, all things are flightier than dreams. One moment only, and death shall supplant them all. But in the light of thy countenance, and in the sweetness of thy beauty, give rest unto him whom thou hast chosen, O merciful Lord Jesus Christ.

Of these two prayers, the first is a devotional work for any occasion when the devout may wish to pray for the dead. The second comes from the funeral service. The passage in the first prayer, "Thou art the God who didst descend into hell and loose the bonds of the captives," refers to what is known in the West as the

Harrowing of Hell. It is believed that with the sin of Adam and Eve the gates of Heaven were shut. The souls of the just were confined in Hell (or Limbo in some versions), while they awaited the coming of the Messiah. After Christ's death on the cross, but before his resurrection on Easter morning, he went down to Hell, brought out these souls, and they entered Heaven.

ISLAMIC FUNERAL PRAYERS

Allahummaghfir li hayyina wa mayyatina wa shahidina wa gha'ibina wa saghirina wa kabirina wa zakarina wa unthana; Allahumma man ahyaitahu minna fa-ahyihee 'alal Islam, wa man tawaffaitahu minna fatawaffahu 'alal Islam.

———

O God! Pardon our living and our dead, the present and the absent, the young and the old, the males and the females. O God! [he/she] to whom Thou accordest life, cause [him/her] to live in the observation of Islam, and [he/she] to whom Thou givest death, cause [him/her] to die in the state of Islam.

Allahummaj'alhu lana fartan waj'alhu lana ajran wa zukhran waj'alhu lana shafi'an wa mushaffa'an.

———

O God! make [him/her] our forerunner, and make [him/her], for us, a reward and a treasure, and make [him/her], for us, a pleader, and accept [his/her] pleading.

At a Muslim funeral, the deceased is placed facing in the direction of the Ka'ba at Mecca, and the imam and the congregation gather around to recite these prayers.

PRAYER TO THE LIVING DEAD WHO ONCE SHARED THIS LIFE

O good and innocent dead, hear us: hear us, you guiding, all-knowing ancestors, you are neither blind nor deaf to this life we live: you did yourselves once share it. Help us therefore for the sake of our devotion, and for our good.

At the beginning of a festival, a leader of the Mende people of Sierra Leone offers this prayer to their departed ancestors, reminding them that they can remember what troubles afflict the living and urging them to help the families and friends they left behind.

SHAKER FUNERAL HYMN

Our sister's gone, she is no more;
She's quit our coast, she's left our shore;
She's burst the bounds of mortal clay,
The spirit's fled and soars away.
We now may hear the solemn call:
"Be ye prepared both great and small;"
The call excludes no sex or age,
For all must quit this mortal stage.
Then let the righteous sing,
When from corruption they get free:
O death where is thy sting?
O grave where is thy victory?

The earliest surviving text for this Shaker hymn is in the 1822 edition of the George DeWitt hymnal of the community at New Lebanon, New York.

Prayers for Help and Protection

HEALTH OF MIND AND BODY

May there be voice in my mouth, breath in my nostrils,
sight in my eyes, hearing in my ears;
may my hair not turn grey or my teeth purple;
may I have much strength in my arms.

May I have power in my thighs, swiftness in my legs,
steadiness in my feet.
May all my limbs be uninjured and my soul remain
unconquered.

Atharva-Veda XIX, 60

Physical health and strength and material prosperity—as well as spiritual and
moral values—are extolled in the Hindu Vedic Code. Taken together, all of these
qualities ennoble human existence.

PRAYER FOR ONE ABOUT TO UNDERGO AN OPERATION

Almighty God our heavenly Father, we beseech thee graciously
to comfort thy servant in his suffering, and to bless the means
made use of for his cure. Fill his heart with confidence, that
though he may be sometime afraid, he yet may put his trust in
thee; through Jesus Christ our Lord. Amen.

In addition to the authorized text for the various liturgies, the Anglican *Book of
Common Prayer* also includes prayers for particular needs, the prayer given above
being one example.

CHARM TO STOP THE FLOW OF BLOOD

The maidens that go yonder, the veins, clothed in red garments, like sisters without a brother, bereft of strength, they shall stand still!

Stand still, thou lower one, stand still, thou higher one; do thou in the middle also stand still! The most tiny vein stands still: may then the great artery also stand still!

Of the hundred arteries, and the thousand veins, those in the middle here have indeed stood still. At the same time the ends have ceased to flow.

Around you has passed a great sandy dike: stand ye still, pray take your ease!

This magical healing charm comes from the Atharva-Veda, Hinduism's second-oldest collection of sacred texts. The bleeding veins are addressed as restless maidens dressed in red robes and commanded to stop. The sandy dike of the final line may refer to a poultice of sand placed on the wound to staunch the flow of blood.

CHARM FOR SEIZURE

I trample on thee, thou seizure,
As tramples whale on brine,
Thou seizure of back, thou seizure of body,
Thou foul wasting of chest

May the strong Lord of life
Destroy thy disease of body
From the crown of thine head
To the base of thy heel;

From thy two loins thither,
From thy two loins hither,
With the power of the Christ of love
And the Creator of the seasons;

With the aid of the Spirit Holy
And the whole Powers together,
With the aid of the Spirit Holy
And the whole Powers together.

Alexander Carmichael reported that among the people of the Scottish islands and Highlands, "chest seizures" (most likely a tubercular ailment) were especially dreaded. This charm would have been recited by a healer as he or she kneaded and massaged the patient's upper body to drive out the seizure.

ANSARI'S MUNAJAT (19)

O God, do not put out this lighted lamp;
Burn not this creature that has been scorched;
Tear not apart this screen that has been sewn;
And do not drive away this newly taught servant.

ANSARI'S MUNAJAT (52)

O God, give us a heart, that we may risk life itself on
Thy way.
And give us a soul that we may devote ourselves to
the other world.

Brevity of expression and intensity of feeling are the hallmarks of the great Afghani scholar, poet, and mystic Khwajih 'Abd Allah Ansari (1006-1088). *Munajat* means "private conversations," and in just a few compact lines the mystic brings his appeal directly to God.

FOR HELP IN SICKNESS

You, Father God,
Who are in the heavens and below;
Creator of everything and omniscient;
Of the earth and the heavens;
We are but little children
Unknowing anything evil;
If this sickness has been brought by man
We beseech you, help us through these roots.
In case it was inflicted by you, the Conserver,
Likewise do we entreat your mercy on your child;
Also you, our grandparents, who sleep in the place of
the shades,
We entreat all of you who sleep on one side.
All ancestors, males and females, great and small,
Help us in this trouble, have compassion on us;
So that we can also sleep peacefully.
And thus do I spit out this mouthful of water!
Pu-pu! Pu-pu!
Please listen to our earnest request.

When sickness comes, all the spirits are invoked for help, from the great Father
God to the least of the ancestors. This prayer of the Luguru people of Tanzania
captures the sense of desperation as death draws near and none of the traditional remedies is working.

A Prayer for the Sick

O Lord, punish me not in thy anger; chastise me not in thy wrath. Have pity on me, O Lord, for I languish away; heal me, O Lord, for my health is shaken. My soul is severely troubled; and thou, O Lord, how long? O Lord, deliver my life once again; save me because of thy grace. For in death there is no thought of thee; in the grave who gives thanks to thee? I am worn out with my groaning; every night I flood my bed with tears; I cause my couch to melt with my weeping. My eye is dimmed from grief; it grows old because of all my foes. Depart from me all you evildoers, for the Lord has heard the sound of my weeping. The Lord has heard my supplication; the Lord receives my prayer. All my foes shall be utterly ashamed and terrified; they shall turn back; they shall be suddenly ashamed.

The Jewish prayer book uses Psalm 6 as a prayer for the sick. Christians will recognize it as the first of the Seven Penitential Psalms.

A Prayer for Courage

Give us grace, O God, to dare to do the deed which we well know cries to be done. Let us not hesitate because of ease, or the words of men's mouths, or our own lives. Mighty causes are calling us—the freeing of women, the training of children, the putting down of hate and murder and poverty—all these and more. But they call with voices that mean work and sacrifice and death. Mercifully grant us, O God, the spirit of Esther, that we say: I will go unto the King and if I perish, I perish. Amen.

W.E.B. Du Bois's allusion to Esther recalls the story of a beautiful Jewish woman who was chosen to be the queen of Ahasuerus, king of Persia (known to history as Xerxes, who reigned 485-464 B.C.E.). The king's vizier, Haman, plotted to destroy in one day all the Jews living in the Persian Empire. When Queen Esther discovered the conspiracy she resolved to go to her husband and plead for the life of her people, although to approach the king unbidden was punishable by death. The entire story is found in the biblical Book of Esther.

To Poseidon before Beginning a Sea Voyage

I begin to sing about Poseidon, the great god, mover of the earth and fruitless sea, god of the deep who is also lord of Helicon and wide Aegae. A two-fold office the gods allotted you, O Shaker of the Earth, to be a tamer of horses and a savior of ships!

Hail, Poseidon, Holder of the Earth, dark-haired lord! O blessed one, be kindly in heart and help those who voyage in ships.

While all three of Poseidon's aspects are presented here, this liturgical hymn asks the god to protect seafarers. As with all of the Homeric hymns, authorship of this prayer is uncertain, but the date is thought to be between the eighth and sixth centuries B.C.E.

May it be thy will, Lord our God, and God of our fathers, to lead us in safety and direct our steps in safety; mayest thou bring us to our destination in life, happiness and peace. Deliver us from every lurking enemy and danger on the road. May we obtain favor, kindness, and love from thee and from all whom we meet. Hear our supplication, for thou art God who hearest prayer and supplication: Blessed art thou, O Lord, who hearest prayer.

Jacob went his way and met the angels of God. On seeing them, Jacob said: "This is God's camp," and he called the name of that place Mahanaim.

I am sending an angel in front of you, to guard you as you go and to guide you to the place I have prepared.

May the Lord bless you and protect you; may the Lord shine his countenance upon you and be gracious to you; may the Lord favor you and grant you peace.

The last three verses of this traveler's prayer are taken from the Torah. The first is from Genesis 32:2-3, the story of Jacob's perilous journey to see Esau, the twin brother he wronged many years before. The second is from Exodus 23:20, in which God promises the Israelites who have escaped from Pharaoh that he will protect them if they keep his commandments. The third and final verse is from Numbers 6:24-26, and is the traditional priestly blessing.

THE PILGRIM'S PRAYER

Along ways of peace and prosperity may the almighty and merciful Lord lead us, and may the Angel Raphael accompany us on the journey. So may we in peace, health, and joy return unto our own.

This prayer of Roman Catholic pilgrims invokes the protection of the angel Raphael, who accompanied Tobias on his travels. The story is found in the Book of Tobias in the Catholic Bible and in the Apocrypha of the Protestant Bible.

PRAYER FOR HOLINESS

Almighty God, giver of all good gifts, whose handiwork is lovely, kindle in our lives the true beauty of holiness, so that graceful by obedience and fair by loving-kindness, we may, through the ripening years, show forth more and more the likeness of thy dear Son Jesus Christ, to whom with thee and Holy Ghost, be all honor and glory, world without end.

This especially lovely prayer comes from a collection published by the Episcopal Church in the United States, *The Offices for Special Occasions*, published in 1929.

Come, Holy Ghost, our hearts inspire,
Let us thine influence prove,
Source of the old prophetic fire,
Fountain of life and love.

Come, Holy Ghost (for moved by thee
The prophets wrote and spoke);
Unlock the truth, thyself the key,
Unseal the sacred book.

Expand thy wings, celestial dove,
Brood o'er our nature's night;
On our disordered spirits move,
And let there now be light.

God through himself we then shall know,
If thou within us shine;
And sound, with all thy saints below,
The depths of love divine.

The preacher John Wesley was the founding genius of Methodism, but its greatest evangelist was John's brother Charles, who based his hymn on a much older Latin one, *Veni, Creator Spiritus*, composed in the ninth century. *Come, Holy Ghost* was first included in Wesley's hymnal of 1740.

Prayer of Saint Thomas Aquinas before Study

Ineffable Creator, who from the treasures of your wisdom have established three hierarchies of angels, have arrayed them in marvelous order above the fiery heavens, and have marshaled the regions of the universe with such artful skill, you are proclaimed the true font of light and wisdom, and the primal origin raised high beyond all things. Pour forth a ray of your brightness into the darkened places of my mind; disperse from my soul the twofold darkness into which I was born: sin and ignorance.

You, who make eloquent the tongues of infants, refine my speech and pour forth upon my lips the goodness of your blessing. Grant to me keenness of mind, capacity to remember, skill in learning, subtlety to interpret, and eloquence in speech. May you guide the beginning of my work, direct its progress, and bring it to completion. You who are true God and true Man, who live and reign, world without end. Amen.

A brilliant theologian and philosopher, Saint Thomas Aquinas also enjoyed a profound spiritual life. This prayer begs for all the qualities a scholar needs.

Two Prayers of Saint Thomas More

I

Give me Thy grace, good Lord,
To set the world at nought;

To set my mind fast upon Thee,
And not to hang upon the blast of men's mouths;

To be content to be solitary;
Not to long for worldly company;

Little and little utterly to cast off the world,
And rid myself of all the business thereof;

Not to long to hear of any worldly things,
But that the hearing of worldly fantasies may be to me
displeasant;

Gladly to be thinking of God,
Piteously to call for His help;

To lean unto the comfort of God,
Busily to labor to love Him;

To know mine own vility and wretchedness,
To humble and meeken myself under the mighty hand of God;

To bewail my sins passed;
For the purging of them patiently to suffer adversity;

Gladly to bear my purgatory here;
To be joyful of tribulations;

To walk the narrow way that leadeth to life,
To bear the cross with Christ;

To have the last thing in remembrance,
To have ever afore mine eye my death that is ever at hand;

To make death no stranger to me,
To foresee and consider the everlasting fire of hell;

To pray for pardon before the judge come,
To have continually in mind the passion that Christ suffered
for me;

For His benefits incessantly to give Him thanks,
To buy the time again that I before have lost;

To abstain from vain confabulations,
To eschew light foolish mirth and gladness;

Recreations not necessary—to cut off;
Of worldly substance, friends, liberty, life and all, to set the
loss at right nought for the winning of Christ:

To think my most enemies my best friends;
For the brethren of Joseph could never have done him so
much good with their love and favor as they did him with
their malice and hatred.

These minds are more to be desired of every man than all the treasure of all the princes and kings, Christian and heathen, were it gathered and laid together all upon one heap.

II

Almighty God, take away from me all vain-glorious minds, all appetites of mine own praise, all envy, covetise, gluttony, sloth, and lechery, all wrathful affections, all appetite of revenging, all desire or delight of other folk's harm, all pleasure in provoking any person to wrath and anger, all delight of exprobation or insultation against any person in their affliction and calamity.

And give me, good Lord, an humble, lowly, quiet, peaceable, patient, charitable, kind, tender, and pitiful mind, with all my works, and all my words, and all my thoughts, to have a taste of thy holy, blessed Spirit.

Give me, good Lord, a full faith, a firm hope, and a fervent charity, a love to the good Lord incomparable above the love to myself; and that I love nothing to thy displeasure, but everything in an order to thee.

Give me, good Lord, a longing to be with thee, not for the avoiding of the calamities of this wretched world, nor so much for the avoiding of the pains of purgatory, nor of the pains of hell neither, nor so much for the attaining of the joys of heaven, in respect of mine own commodity, as even for a very love to thee.

Take from me, good Lord, this lukewarm fashion, or rather key-cold manner of meditation, and this dullness in praying unto thee. And give me warmth, delight and quickness in thinking upon thee. And give me thy grace to long for thine holy sacraments, and specially to rejoice in the presence of thy very blessed body, Sweet Savior Christ, in the holy sacrament of the altar, and duly to thank thee for thy gracious visitation therewith, and at that high memorial, with tender compassion, to remember and consider thy most bitter passion.

Make us all, good Lord, virtually participant of that holy sacrament this day, and every day make us all lively members, sweet Savior Christ, of thine holy mystical body, thy Catholic Church.

The things, good Lord, that I pray for, give me thy grace to labor for. Amen.

Saint Thomas More (1478-1535) composed these prayers in 1534 and 1535 respectively, while he was imprisoned in the Tower of London for his refusal to acknowledge Henry VIII as supreme head of the Church in England.

The first prayer, "Give me Thy grace good Lord," he wrote in charcoal in the margins of his prayer book, all paper and ink having been taken away from him. The second prayer he composed sometime between July 1, 1535, the day he received the death sentence, and July 6, 1535, the day he was executed.

I

Teach me, O God, not to torture myself, not to make a martyr out of myself through stifling reflection, but rather teach me to breathe deeply in faith.

II

Father in Heaven! Show unto us a little patience; for we often intend in all sincerity to commune with Thee and yet we speak in such a foolish fashion. Sometimes, when we judge that what has come to us is good, we do not have enough words to thank Thee; just as a mistaken child is thankful for having gotten his own way. Sometimes things go so badly that we call upon Thee; we even complain and cry unto Thee; just as an unreasoning child fears what would do him good. Oh, but if we are so childish how far from being true children of Thine who art our true Father, ah, as if an animal would pretend to have man as a father. How childish we are and how little our proposals and language resemble the language which we ought to use with Thee, we understand at least that it ought not to be thus and that we ought to be otherwise. Have then a little patience with us.

To Søren Kierkegaard (1813-1855), Denmark's Lutheran Church was a domesticated arm of the state, and most Danish Christians were dull and lacking in religious fervor. In these prayers, as in all his writings, Kierkegaard tries to shake conventional Christians out of their complacency by addressing God in a way that is direct and familiar.

A Prayer of W.E.B. Du Bois

Once they tell us, Jehovah, that in the great shadows of the past Thou hast whispered to a quivering people, saying, "Be not afraid." He watching over Israel slumbers not nor sleeps. Grant us today, O God, that fearlessness that rests on confidence in the ultimate rightness of things. Let us not be afraid neither of mere physical hurt, nor of the unfashionableness of our color, nor of the unpopularity of our cause; let us turn toward the battle of life undismayed and above all when we have fought the good fight grant us to face the shadow of death with the same courage that has let us live. Amen.

This particular prayer was inspired by Du Bois's reading of Psalm 121.

For Protection against Danger

Make haste, O Christ our God, and go before us lest we be overcome by the enemy who blaspheme thee and maltreat us: destroy by the virtue of thy Cross those who war against us, that they may know the might of the Orthodox faith, at the prayers of the Mother of God, O Lover of men.

There is a martial tone to this Eastern Orthodox prayer in which Christ is imagined as a warrior who uses his Cross as a weapon to scatter the enemies of the faithful.

Saint Patrick's Breastplate

I arise today
Through a mighty strength, the invocation of the Trinity.
Through a belief in the threeness,
Through a confession of the oneness
Of the Creator of creation.

I arise today
Through the strength of Christ's birth with his baptism,
Through the strength of his crucifixion with his burial,
Through the strength of his resurrection with his ascension,
Through the strength of his descent for the judgment of Doom.

I arise today
Through the strength of the love of cherubim,
In obedience of angels,
In the service of archangels,
In hope of resurrection to meet with reward,
In prayers of patriarchs,
In predictions of prophets,
In preachings of apostles,
In faith of confessors,
In innocence of holy virgins,
In deeds of righteous men.

I arise today
Through the strength of heaven:
Light of sun
Radiance of moon,
Splendor of fire,

Speed of lightning,
Swiftness of wind,
Depth of sea,
Stability of earth,
Firmness of rock.

I arise today
Through God's strength to pilot me:
God's might to uphold me,
God's wisdom to guide me,
God's eye to look before me,
God's ear to hear me,
God's word to speak for me,
God's hand to guard me,
God's way to lie before me,
God's shield to protect me,
God's host to save me
From snares of devils,
From temptations of vices,
From everyone who shall wish me ill,
Afar and near,
Alone and in a multitude.

I summon today all these powers between me and those evils,
Against every cruel merciless power that may oppose my
body and soul,
Against incantations of false prophets,
Against black laws of pagandom,
Against false laws of heretics,
Against spells of enchantresses and smiths and wizards,
Against every knowledge that corrupts man's body and soul.

Christ shield me today
Against poison, against burning,
Against drowning, against wounding,
So that there may come to me abundance of reward,
Christ with me, Christ before me, Christ behind me;
Christ in me, Christ beneath me, Christ above me;
Christ on my right, Christ on my left,
Christ when I lie down, Christ when I sit down,
Christ when I arise.
Christ in the heart of every man who thinks of me.
Christ in the mouth of everyone who speaks of me.
Christ in every eye that sees me,
Christ in every ear that hears me.

I arise today
Through a mighty strength, the invocation of the Trinity.
Through a belief in the threeness,
Through a confession of the oneness
Of the Creator of creation.

In spite of its attribution, no one knows with any certainty if Saint Patrick
(c. 389-c. 461 C.E.), the Apostle to the Irish, composed this prayer. Early Celtic
literature, pagan and Christian, is filled with examples of incantations and prayers
such as this which were believed to protect travelers. The name "breastplate" is a
translation of the Latin term *lorica* and recalls the protective quality of these
chants. In some Irish manuscripts, Saint Patrick's Breastplate is called "The Song
of the Deer," a reference to the legend that God once transformed Patrick and his
companions into a herd of deer to save them from enemies who were about to
overtake them.

Prayer for Averting Death

Homage, Rudra, to thy wrath and thy arrow,
and homage to thy two arms.

Look on us, Rudra, kind One, with that form of thine which
is beneficent,
that form of thine, O Rover on the Mountain, which is most
blissful.

The arrow, O Rover on the Mountain, that thou holdest in
thy hand to shoot,
make it beneficent for us, Mountain Lord, destroy not man
nor a moving thing.

Mountain Lord, we speak to thee with blissful words so that
all that is moving [and living]
may, free from disease, have happiness of heart.

He has spoken in defense of us, the Advocate,
the first Divine Physician.
Subdue all the serpents and send away the Yatudhanis down
below.

Having unbent thy bow, and dulled the points of thy arrows,
thou, thousand-eyed, hundred-quivered,
be benevolent and gracious to us.

Slay not, O Rudra, either the great or the small,
either the growing or the fully grown,
slay neither a father nor a mother,
nor, Rudra, do thou injure our own dear body.

Injure not either our sons or our grandsons,
or our own life, or our cattle, or our horses;
and slay not our heroes when they are filled with wrath.
We shall with oblations ever call on thee.

~

Thou who makest people flee,
thou, Lord of Soma juice,
thou Cleaver, blue and red,
don't threaten any of our children,
or any of our animals;
let nothing of ours be sick.

To Rudra, the powerful who has braided hair,
to the Ruler of heroes, we bring these our hymns,
so it may be well with our bipeds and quadrupeds,
and in this village all be well-fed, all undiseased.

That aspect of thine, Rudra, which is
benign, always benign and healing,
is benign, and heals disease,
with that be gracious, so we may live.

May that missile of Rudra pass us by, and
the wrath of the impetuous One, ready to destroy.
Turn, bounteous One, thy strong bow from our heroes,
and be gracious to our sons and grandsons.

Thou most bounteous, most benign,
be beneficent and loving to us.

Lay down thy weapon on the remotest tree,
and clad in thy robe of skin,
and bearing thy Pinaka, come!

Yajur-Veda V, 16

Although Siva (also known in the West as Shiva) is the Destroyer with a host of terrifying attributes, it is the Deva Rudra who is the personification of death. Nonetheless, in this Veda, Rudra and Siva share some of the same attributes: the title Mountain Lord, the blue and red skin, and the bow Pinaka (which in later myths became the proper name of Siva's personal bow).

The petitioner begs Rudra to put aside his destructive temper and come with only his benign attributes. The people will have nothing to fear if he leaves his arrow beneath a remote tree and comes to them with only his bow.

AN ANABAPTIST HYMN

My eternal Lord and Father
I am your poor, unworthy child
Teach me and make me know
So that I can observe your ways
That is my truest desire.

To walk in your strength in death
Through tribulation, martyrdom, fear and need
Keep me in your strength
That I may never again be separated
From your love, O God.

There are many who travel this path
On which stands the cup of suffering
And also much false doctrine
With which they try to turn us away
From Christ our Lord.

I lift up my soul to you, Lord
I hope in you in times of danger
Let me not become a disgrace
So that my enemies have the victory
Over me on this earth.

They have me here locked up.
I wait, O God, from my heart
With great desire
If you would only stir
And save your ones in prison.

Detested by both Catholics and mainstream Protestants, the Anabaptists found no safe haven in the sixteenth century. They were imprisoned, often tortured, and martyred in the most gruesome fashion throughout Europe. These verses, taken from a longer hymn, were written by Annelein of Freiberg (1512?-1529). To mock her belief in the rebaptism of adults, she was nearly drowned, then hauled out of the water and burned at the stake. The Amish have preserved this hymn in the *Ausbund*, a collection of the oldest hymns of the Swiss Anabaptists.

PROTECTION AGAINST SNAKE BITE

When the foot in the night
Stumbles against the obstacle that shrinks and rears and bites,
Let, O Snake, thou our Father, Father of our tribe,
We are thy sons,
Let it be a branch that rears and strikes,
But not one of thy sharp-toothed children,
O Father of the tribe, we are thy sons.

The Pygmies of Zaire offer this prayer to the snake-guardian of their tribe, asking him to protect his human children from his snake children.

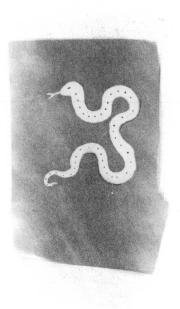

A Woman's Prayer

O quick; defend me from the claws of the dog, from the unicorns' horns, and I will praise you, my God, among my brethren, in the assembly. At the request of your martyrs Sabbatius, Probatius, Stephen and Cyriacus, protect your servant, gracious God; rid her of every weakness in her soul. For it is through the name of the Lord, the living God, that salvation comes.

Many have been at pains to set forth the history of what time has brought to fulfillment among us.
A record of the ancestry from which Jesus Christ was born.
At the beginning of time the Word already was, and God had the Word abiding with him, and the Word was God.
Saint Phocas, Saint Mercurius, protect your servant.

An Egyptian papyrus of the fifth or sixth century C.E. records this prayer of an anonymous Christian woman. To ward off evil, she invokes her favorite saints, but also, in the second part of her prayer, recites the opening lines of the gospels of Luke, Matthew, and John as a kind of holy charm.

BLESSING OF BRIGIT

Brigit daughter of Dugall the Brown
Son of Aodh son of Art son of Conn
Son of Criara son of Cairbre son of Cas
Son of Cormac son of Cartach son of Conn.

Each day and each night
That I say the Descent of Brigit.

I shall not be slain,
I shall not be sworded,
I shall not be put in a cell,
I shall not be hewn,
I shall not be riven,
I shall not be anguished,
I shall not be wounded,
I shall not be ravaged,
I shall not be blinded,
I shall not be made naked,
I shall not be left bare,
Nor will Christ
Leave me forgotten.

Nor fire shall burn me,
Nor sun shall burn me,
Nor moon shall blanch me.

Nor water shall drown me,
Nor flood shall drown me,
Nor brine shall drown me.

Nor seed of fairy host shall lift me,
Nor seed of airy host shall lift me,
Nor earthly being destroy me.

I am under the shielding
Of good Brigit each day;
I am under the shielding
Of good Brigit each night.

I am under the keeping
Of the Nurse of Mary,
Each early and late,
Every dark, every light.

Brigit is my comrade-woman,
Brigit is my maker of song,
Brigit is my helping-woman,
My choicest of women, my guide.

Saint Brigit or Brigid or Bride is the most important of the Celtic female saints and is blessed with an especially rich collection of legends. One says she was the midwife of the Blessed Virgin Mary, helping to deliver the Christ Child. Another says that she nursed the infant Jesus at her own breast. After Mary herself, no woman saint in Heaven was considered a more powerful protector than Saint Brigid.

In the Scottish Highlands and islands, the Genealogy, or Descent, of Brigit was used as a charm to protect the believer from all the forces of nature and the malice of human and supernatural enemies. Saint Brigid's feast day is February 1.

Prayers for Prosperity

To Welcome Raided Cattle into the Fenced Homestead

The cattle, my! come into this house which is warm.
And do not ye say: "We are few."
Ye come slowly and ye stay quietly.

Throughout Africa, cattle, sheep, goats, and even children are a sign of a family's prosperity and good fortune. This invocation comes from the Nandi people of Kenya, a tribe that is renowned for its cattle-raiding exploits.

Milking Croon

Come, Mary, and milk my cow,
Come, Bride, and encompass her,
Come Columba the benign,
And twine thine arms around my cow.
Ho my heifer, ho my gentle heifer,
Ho my heifer, ho my gentle heifer,
Ho my heifer, ho my gentle heifer,
My heifer dear, generous and kind,
For the sake of the High King take to thy calf.

Come, Mary Virgin, to my cow,
Come, great Bride, the beauteous,

Come, thou milkmaid of Jesus Christ,
And place thine arms beneath my cow.
Ho my heifer, ho my gentle heifer.

Lovely black cow, pride of the shieling,
First cow of the byre, choice mother of calves,
Wisps of straw round the cows of the townland,
A shackle of silk on my heifer beloved.
Ho my heifer, ho my gentle heifer.

My black cow, my black cow,
A like sorrow afflicts me and thee,
Thou grieving for thy lovely calf,
I for my beloved son under the sea,
My beloved only son under the sea.

In the legends of the Celts, the Blessed Virgin Mary, Saint Bride (or Brigid) and
Saint Columba are all associated with milk. Mary is said to have bathed the
Christ Child in milk during their journey to Egypt. Saint Brigid's cows were
famous for producing a whole lake of milk every day. And Saint Columba once
came to the aid of a widow whose cow would not give milk. The shieling referred
to in the prayer is a rough hut built near the pasture where cattle graze.

To the Earth, Forest, and Rivers at the Sowing Season

O Earth, wherever it be my people dig, be kindly to them. Be fertile when they give the little seeds to your keeping. Let your generous warmth nourish them and your abundant moisture germinate them. Let them swell and sprout, drawing life from you, and burgeon under your fostering care: and soon we shall redden your bosom with the blood of goats slain in your honor, and offer to you the first fruits of your munificence, first fruits of millet and oil of sesame, of gourds and cucumbers and deep-mashed melons.

O trees of forest and glade, fall easily under the ax. Be gentle to my people. Let no harm come to them. Break no limb in your anger. Crush no one in your displeasure. Be obedient to the woodsman's wishes and fall as he would have you fall, not perversely or stubbornly, but as his ax directs. Submit yourselves freely to my people, as this tree has submitted itself to me. The ax rings, it bites into the tough wood. The tree totters and falls. The lightning flashes, its fire tears at the heart of the wood. The tree totters and falls. Before the lightning the tree falls headlong, precipitate, knowing neither direction nor guidance. But the woodsman guides the tree where he wills and lays it to rest gently and with deliberation. Fall, O trees of forest and glade, even as this tree has fallen, hurting no one, obedient, observant of my will.

O rivers and streams, where the woodsman has laid bare the earth, where he has hewn away the little bushes and torn out encumbering grass, there let your waters overflow. Bring down the leafy mold from the forest and the fertilizing silt from the mountains. When the rains swell your banks, spread out your waters and lay your rich treasures on our gardens.

Conspire together, O earth and rivers: conspire together O earth and rivers and forests. Be gentle and give us plenty from your teeming plenty.

A chief of the Didinga people in the Sudan offers this magnificent prayer to the earth, the forest, and the rivers, addressing these aspects of the natural world as intelligent beings. In the Didinga worldview, nature cannot be ordered to behave as humans would like but must be appeased with sacrifices and begged not to hurt the tribe or the crops.

MENOMINEE PRAYER TO THE THUNDERBIRDS

You Thunderers are our eldest brothers! Now we have asked you to come with your rain to water our gardens, freshen our lives, and ward off disease. We beg you not to bring with you your terrible hail and wind. You have four degrees of tempest, come with a moderate rain and not a deluge. Do not bring too much lightning. Grant this, that we may be happy till the next time of offering. This tobacco we offer you, you can see it before us. It is for you.

This is a liturgical prayer, offered by the leader of the tribe to the Thunderers or Thunderbirds at a public rite to mark the beginning of the growing season. The Thunderers are mythical other-than-human figures. Once they were the ancestors of the tribe; now they are the Menominee's guardian spirits.

THE PRAYER OF ABRAHAM

My Lord! Make this a region of security and bestow upon its people fruits, such of them as believe in Allah and the Last day. . . .

Our Lord! Accept from us [this duty]. Lo! Thou, only Thou, art the Hearer, the Knower.

Our Lord! Make us submissive unto Thee and of our seed a nation submissive unto Thee, and show us our ways of worship, and relent toward us. Lo! Thou, only Thou, are the Relenting, the Merciful.

Our Lord! And raise up in their midst a messenger from among them who will recite unto them Thy revelations, and shall instruct them in the Scripture and in wisdom and shall make them grow. Lo! Thou, only Thou, art the Mighty, Wise.

Sura II, 126, 127-29

In the Sura of the Cow, Abraham offers this prayer to Allah as he and his son Ishmael stand in the foundations of the house that will become the Ka'ba of Mecca. According to the Qur'an, Muslims have the fullness of revelation, but Jews and Christians are also rightly guided because they possess (albeit incompletely) the faith of Abraham.

PRAYER FOR RAIN

Blessed art thou, Lord our God and God of our fathers, God of Abraham, God of Isaac, God of Jacob; great, mighty and revered God, sublime God, who bestowest loving kindness, and art Master of all things; who rememberest the good deeds of our fathers, and who wilt graciously bring a redeemer to their children's children for the sake of thy name. O King, Supporter, Savior and Shield!

Af-Bri is the title of the prince of rain,
Who gathers the clouds and makes them drop rain,
Water to adorn the earth with verdure.
Be it not held back because of unpaid debts;
O shield faithful Israel who prays for rain.

Blessed art thou, O Lord, Shield of Abraham.
Thou, O Lord, art mighty forever; thou revivest the dead; thou art powerful to save.

May he send rain from the heavenly source,
To soften the earth with its crystal drops.
Thou hast named water the symbol of thy might;
Its drops refresh all that have breath of life,
And revive those who praise thy powers of rain.

On the eighth day of Sukkoth, the Jewish harvest festival, this prayer for rain is chanted. The prayer is lengthy and goes on to remind God of the kindness he showed to Abraham, Isaac, Jacob, the Twelve Tribes, Moses and Aaron, and of the miracles he performed for them through water. Portions of this prayer were written by Rabbi Elazar ha-Kallir in the seventh century C.E.

A Merchant's Prayer for Wealth

I arouse Indra, the Merchant,

may he come to us and be our Guide,

Driving out the malevolent, the robber and wild beasts;

may he, the mighty, give me wealth.

Indra is a Hindu god who is venerated as a divine guide for all endeavors that take place outside the home. The merchant of the prayer suggests that Indra is also a member of the merchant class as a way of establishing a closer identification with the god.

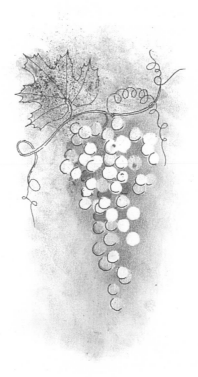

A Prayer for Success in Gambling

The successful, victorious, skillfully gaming Apsara, that Apsara who makes the winnings in the game of dice, do I call hither.

The skillfully gaming Apsara who sweeps and heaps up the stakes, that Apsara who takes the winnings in the game of dice, do I call hither.

May she, who dances about with the dice, when she desires to win for us, obtain the advantage by her magic! May she come to us full of abundance! Let them not win this wealth of ours!

The Apsaras who rejoice in dice, who carry grief and wrath—that joyful and exalting Apsara, do I call hither.

This prayer or charm comes from the Atharva-Veda, a collection of sacred texts second in antiquity only to the Rig-Veda. Among the hymns and prayers of the Atharva-Veda are a few magical incantations. This prayer for success at dice seems to be among the magic charms. The Apsaras invoked in the prayer are divine nymphs, members of the incredibly crowded Hindu pantheon.

Prayers of War and Peace

A Warrior's Prayer to Ares

Ares, exceeding in strength, chariot-rider, golden-helmed, doughty in heart, shield-bearer, Savior of cities, harnessed in bronze, strong of arm, unwearying, mighty with the spear, O defense of Olympus, father of warlike Victory, ally of Themis, stern governor of the rebellious, leader of righteous men, sceptered King of manliness, who whirl your fiery sphere among the planets in their sevenfold courses through the ether wherein your blazing steeds ever bear you above the third firmament of heaven; hear me, helper of men, giver of dauntless youth! Shed down a kindly ray from above upon my life, and strength of war, that I may be able to drive away bitter cowardice from my head and crush down the deceitful impulses of my soul. Restrain also the keen fury of my heart which provokes me to tread the ways of blood-curdling strife. Rather, O blessed one, give you me boldness to abide within the harmless laws of peace, avoiding strife and hatred and the violent fiends of death.

Of the entire collection known as the Homeric hymns, this invocation to Ares, god of war, is the only individualized devotional prayer. The thirty-three hymns themselves are of an uncertain date, and may or may not have been composed by Homer.

At a War Ritual around the Sacred Rock

We are poured on the enemy like a mighty torrent;
We are poured like a river in spate when the rain is in the
mountains.
The water hisses down the sands, swirling, exultant, and the
tree that stood in its path is torn up quivering.
It is tossed from eddy to eddy.
We are poured on the enemy and they are bewildered.
They look this way and that seeking escape, but our spears
fall thickly about them.
Our spears cling to their bodies and they are routed.
They look this way and that for deliverance, but they cannot
escape us, the avengers, the great killers.
God of our fathers, guide our spears, our spears which thy
lilac has touched.
They are anointed with sacrifice, with the sacrifice of
unblemished kids, consecrated and hallowed. . . .
Help us, high spirit. Slay with us.
Let death come to their ranks, let the villages mourn their
lost warriors.
Let their villages be desolate, let them echo with the cry of
mourning.
We shall return rejoicing; and the lowing of cattle is in our ears.
The lowing of innumerable cattle will make glad our hearts.

Praying around their sacred rock, the Didinga of Sudan describe in vivid terms a
great victory over their enemies. Then, afraid that they may appear too proud,
they beg for God's help and sacrifice to God with the same spears they will use
against their enemies.

War Songs of the Menominee

The warrior of the sacred bundle now starts.
As he walks he is seeking for the enemy.

These things we use are truly of god power,
Powerful are the things we use
God said to us they shall be powerful.

Where I volunteer to fight
As I am walking along.

Savage I am
As God I am.

Brave I am called.

I myself, I am surely,
Over and over, God, I am.

Before the Menominee went to war, warriors brought out the sacred bundle that held the tribe's talismans and carried it in procession through the village. A dog was sacrificed and eaten in the bundle's presence, and then tobacco was offered to it. Finally, the war dance began, with the warriors boasting of their savagery and courage.

The final two lines of the war song is a chant the leader of the war party sang just before attacking the enemy. The Menominee preferred to attack just before daybreak, when men sleep most soundly. The chant was believed to overwhelm the enemy with an even more profound sleep.

Aztec War Song

There, where the darts are dyed,
where the shields are painted,
are the perfumed white flowers,
flowers of the heart.
The flowers of the Giver of Life
open their blossoms.
Their perfume is sought by the lords:
this is Tenochtitlán.

Death is here among the flowers,
in the midst of the plain!
Close to the war,
when the war begins,
in the midst of the plain;
the dust rises as if it were smoke,
entangled and twisted round
with the flowery strands of death . . .
Be not afraid, my heart!
In the midst of the plain
my heart craves death
by the sharpness of the obsidian blades.
This is all my heart craves:
death in war . . .

From where the eagles rest,
from where the ocelots are exalted,
The Sun is invoked.

Like a shield that descends,
so does the Sun set.
In Mexico night is falling,
war rages on all sides.
O Giver of Life!
war draws near . . .

Proud of itself
is the city of Mexico Tenochtitlán.
Here no one fears to die in war.
This is our glory.
This is Your command,
O Giver of Life!
Keep this is mind, O princes,
do not forget it.
Who could conquer Tenochtitlán?
Who could shake the foundation of the heavens?
Through our arrows,
through our shields,
the city exists.
Mexico-Tenochtitlán remains.

The Aztecs were a warrior nation that conquered and held in subjection most of the other nations and tribes of Central America. Their warriors developed a kind of military mysticism in which they compared themselves to the eagle and the ocelot. Like these totemic animals, Aztec warriors were swift, strong, and lethal. The Aztecs exulted in their success ("Who could conquer Tenochtitlán?"), but eventually it proved to be their undoing. When Hernán Cortés landed in Mexico in 1521, the Aztecs' neighbors allied themselves with the Spaniards, and together they destroyed the city of Tenochtitlán.

THE CITY OF UNION WAR SONG

Behold it is a time of war
And we have been enlisting,
Emmanuel we're fighting for
And Satan we're resisting.
We have not in this war begun
To turn our backs as traitors
But we will all unite as one
Against our carnal natures.

Mother Ann Lee, who founded the Shakers, was often seen as a warrior against Satan and sin. Out of that tradition grew the genre of Shaker "war songs." At the City of Union community in Enfield, Connecticut, the brothers and sisters wielded invisible spiritual swords as they danced and sang this hymn.

VICTORY IN BATTLE

Breaker of hurdles, finder of light, thunder-armed,
he triumphs in battle, crushing the foe with his might.
Follow him brothers! Quit yourselves like heroes!
Emulate Indra in prowess, my comrades!

Ours be Indra when our banners are gathered!
May the arrows that are ours be victorious,
and our heroes rise superior to all!
Protect us, ye Devas! in the battle.

Go forward, warriors! and conquer.
May Indra give you protection!
Valiant be your arms, so that
you become invincible.

Rig-Veda X, 103

Indra, the Supreme Hero, is the national god of the Vedic Hindus. His eternal enemy is Vritra, who strives to imprison the sun and keep the world in darkness. In one of his cosmic battles against Vritra, Indra smashed the barricade that imprisoned the sun and brought light back to the world.

An Embattled People's Prayer to Athena

Of Pallas Athena, guardian of the city, I begin to sing. Dread is she, and with Ares she loves deeds of war, the sack of cities and the shouting and the battle. It is she who saves the people as they go out to war and come back.

Hail, goddess, and give us good fortune with happiness!

This is a liturgical hymn that may have been sung to Athena in her temple, the Parthenon, in Athens. Like all of the Homeric hymns, the date and authorship of this prayer is uncertain.

Peace in All Things

The peace in the sky, the peace in the mid-air,
the peace on the earth, the peace in the waters,
the peace in the plants, the peace in the forest trees,
the peace in All Devas, the peace in Brahman,
the peace in all things
the peace in peace—
may that peace come to me!

In Hinduism, the Devas are Divine Manifestations, both male and female. This prayer for peace calls upon all the gods, as well as Brahman—the Divine Essence, or Brahma as he is also known—to grant the petitioner perfect peace.

PRAYER FOR PEACE

O God, from whom proceed all holy desires, right counsels, and just works, give to your servants that peace which the world cannot give; that our hearts may be disposed to obey your commandments, and the fear of enemies being removed, our times, by your protection, may be peaceful. Through Our Lord Jesus Christ, your Son, who lives and reigns with you in the unity of the Holy Spirit, one God, forever and ever. Amen.

This ancient and very beautiful prayer comes from the Roman Catholic Votive Mass for Peace.

Behold, how good and pleasant it is
for brethren to dwell together in unity!
It is like the precious ointment upon the head,
that ran down upon the beard,
even Aaron's beard:
that went down to the skirts of his garments;
As the dew of Hermon,
and as the dew that descended
upon the mountains of Zion:
for there the Lord commanded the blessing,
even life for evermore.

Although brief, this psalm is rich in imagery that evokes the abundant blessings of peace. Peace is like holy oil that consecrates a high priest (Aaron, the brother of Moses, being the prototype of all high priests), or the waters that cascade down the slopes of Mount Hermon, a snowcapped mountain far to the north of Jerusalem.

The Priest's Prayer for Peace

Libera nos, quaesumus, Domine, ab omnibus malis, praeteritis, praesentibus, et futuris; et intercedente beata et gloriosa semper Virgine Dei Genitrice Maria, cum beatis Apostolis tuis Petro et Paulo, atque Andrea, et omnibus Sanctis, da propitius pacem in diebus nostris, ut ope misericordiae tuae adjuti, et a peccato simus semper liberi, et ab omni perturbatione securi. Per eumdem Dominum nostrum Jesum Christum Filium tuum. Qui tecum vivit et regnat in unitate Spiritus Sancti Deus per omnia secula seculorum. Amen.

Pax Domini sit semper vobiscum.

Et cum spiritu tuo.

——

Deliver us, we beseech you, O Lord, from all evils, past, present, and to come; and by the intercession of the blessed and glorious Mary, ever Virgin, Mother of God, together with your blessed Apostles Peter and Paul, and Andrew, and all the saints, grant of your goodness peace in our days, that aided by the riches of your mercy, we may be always free from sin and safe from all disturbance. Through the same our Lord, Jesus Christ, your Son, who lives and reigns with you in the unity of the Holy Spirit, God, world without end. Amen.

May the peace of the Lord be with you always.

And with your spirit.

In the Roman Catholic Mass, before Communion is given to the faithful, the priest takes the Sacred Host—the bread that has been transubstantiated to the Body and Blood of Jesus Christ—and begs God to grant peace to the assembled congregation, the Church, and the whole world.

Prayer in Time of Trouble

Let us pray to the Lord.

Lord have mercy.

(make the Sign of the Cross) O Lord of Powers, be with us, for in the time of trouble we have no other help but You. O Lord, God of Powers, have mercy on us.

O God, our help in time of need, Who are good and merciful, and Who inclines to the supplication of His people, look down upon us, miserable sinners, have mercy on us, and deliver us from the trouble that now besets us, for which we acknowledge we are deservedly suffering.

We acknowledge and believe, O Lord, that all the trials of this life are disposed by You for our chastisement, when we drift away from You, and disobey Your commandments. Deal with us not according to our iniquities, but according to your manifold mercies, for we are the works of Your hands, and You know our weaknesses.

Grant, we beseech You, Your divine helping Grace, and endow us with patience and strength to endure our tribulations with complete submission to Your Will.

You know our misery and sufferings, and to You, our only hope and refuge, we flee for relief and comfort, trusting in Your infinite love and compassion, that in due time, when You know best, You will deliver us from this trouble, and turn our distress to comfort, when we shall rejoice in Your mercy, and exalt and praise Your Holy Name *(make the Sign of the Cross)* O Father, Son and Holy Spirit, both now and ever, and unto ages of ages. Amen.

While many prayers beg God to shield his people from trouble, this Eastern Orthodox prayer is designed to console the faithful after some adversity has already arrived.

The Meditation of Chenresig

HEREIN IS CONTAINED THAT WHICH BENEFITS
EVERYONE THROUGHOUT THE HEAVENS

I take refuge in the Great Awakening
And its unfolding
Within these exalted forms
Until I realize complete enlightenment.

May performance of all virtues
Bring auspicious fate.
Only for benefit of all
May the truth be finally perceived.

At all times from the crown of the head
Of all sentient beings
Throughout the heavens
Blossoms a white lotus
Supporting a lunar disc,
Above which appears
The White Seed Syllable HRI,
The embodiment of the highest,
The glorious divinity Chenresig,
The one of all-perceiving compassion
From whose body shines the pure and clear
Five-colored rainbowed rays.
His all seeing eyes radiate compassion
From a beautiful and smiling face.

Of his four arms, the first pair
Are palm to palm in prayer,
The lower two hold a crystal rosary
On the right, and a white lotus on the left.
He is adorned with precious raiment,
Jewels and fur of the wild beast
About his shoulders,
Glorified by the Buddha of the Boundless Light
Shining forth from the crown of his head.

He sits with crossed legs
In the position of Immutability.
He rests his back upon
The Stainless Moon of Void.
All Deities of Refuge
Are manifest in his changes.

O noble One of pure white form
Crowned with Complete Awareness,
Whose compassionate eyes perceive all Being,
Let all Reverence be paid to Chenresig!

Now from my prayer
Arises the single-minded
Mind of Meditation.

All form is radiance and wisdom
Cleansing the illusion-mind from all impurities.
Now this very world itself
Is known to be the Pure Land of Perfect Bliss.
All beings born of essence—and void—

Have body, speech, and mind
By Chenresig's Blessing
These three are seen to be
The illumination of the void.
Realizing the essential emptiness of all existence,
Ignorance and wisdom, as well as all appearances,
Are known as illusion
And harmony prevails.
OM MANI PADME HUM
HAIL THE JEWEL IN THE LOTUS

In Tibetan Buddhism, Chenresig is the name for Avalokitesvara, the disciple of Gautama Buddha who dedicated himself to the salvation of all living creatures. He is also widely known as the Buddha of Compassion and is venerated as the greatest of the Bodhisattvas—those who have sought Enlightenment not for their own glory but for the benefit of all beings.

Meditation is, of course, essential to all Buddhist sects; it is the way that leads to Enlightenment, which is the discovery of one's own true nature.

This meditation is drawn from the Kriya Tantra of Tibetan Buddhism. As a purification meditation, its primary goal is to help the practitioner draw nearer to the Buddha by cleansing all negatives from the mind, body, and speech. At the same time, by meditating on the compassionate Chenresig, the believer develops the Bodhicitta, or Enlightened Mind, filled with compassion for all living things.

OM MANI PADME HUM is the mantra for this meditation, and the believer is urged to repeat it 108 times, all the while visualizing the HRI Seed Syllable, which expresses the essence of the mantra. The light that emanates from HRI will dissolve all physical forms and even human thoughts until the believer perceives that HRI is the only thing that has existence. When even HRI diminishes and disappears from the contemplative's mind, then he or she has drawn close to Enlightenment, or the One True State.

Prayer for Our Enemies

Thou who didst pray for them that crucified thee, O Lord, Lover of the souls of men, and who didst command thy servants to pray for their enemies, forgive those who hate and maltreat us, and turn our lives from harm and evil to brotherly love and good works: for this we humbly bring our prayer, that with one accord and one heart we may glorify thee who alone lovest mankind.

As thy first martyr Stephen prayed to thee for his murderers, O Lord, so we fall before thee and pray: forgive all who hate and maltreat us and let none of them perish because of us, but all be saved by thy grace, O God the all-bountiful.

This Eastern Orthodox prayer alludes to the martyrdom of Saint Stephen. The Apostles appointed Saint Stephen a deacon for the Church in Jerusalem. His zeal offended some of the Jews of the city, who dragged him outside the walls and stoned him to death. His final words were, "Lord, lay not this sin to their charge." The full story of Stephen is found in the Acts of the Apostles 6 and 7.

Prayers to Holy Beings

To the Most Holy Mother of God

Queen, thou holdest in thy arms the all-ruling Son of God—Child of thine, dread of the Angels. Make Him merciful in His counsels toward men. Protect and guard the whole world from woe.

This Greek invocation to the Blessed Virgin Mary is from "The Christian Epigrams," a monumental collection of prayers found inscribed on the walls of churches throughout the old Byzantine Empire. The date of this prayer is uncertain, although it may be as early as the seventh century.

The Memorare

Remember, O most gracious Virgin Mary, that never was it known that anyone who fled to thy protection, implored thy help, or sought thy intercession was left unaided. Inspired by this confidence, I fly unto thee, O Virgin of virgins, my Mother. To thee come, before thee I stand, sinful and sorrowful. O Mother of the Word Incarnate, despise not my petitions but in thy mercy hear and answer me. Amen.

Until the nineteenth century, this prayer to the Virgin Mary was virtually unknown in the English-speaking world. An English priest, Reverend Ambrose Saint John, translated it into English, and its popularity spread throughout Great Britain to the United States. Although the Memorare is commonly attributed to Saint Bernard of Clairvaux, it is in fact derived from a fifteenth-century Latin hymn.

From the Sura of the Cow

Who is an enemy to Gabriel! For he it is who hath revealed
[this Scripture] to thy heart by Allah's leave, confirming that
which was [revealed] before it, and a guidance and glad tidings
to believers; Who is an enemy to Allah, and to His angels and
His messengers, and Gabriel and Michael! Then, lo! Allah
[himself] is an enemy to the disbelievers.

Verily We have revealed unto thee clear tokens, and only
miscreants will disbelieve in them.

Sura II, 97-99

Gabriel is the angel who brought Allah's revelation (the Qur'an) to Muhammad.
In Islamic cosmology, there are many angels in Heaven who worship Allah and
do his bidding. While it is true that Islam forbids believers to ask angels to intercede for them, nonetheless angels must be respected, especially the angel Gabriel,
the primary messenger of Allah's revelation.

The Akathist Hymn to Our Lady

Hail, for through thee joy shall shine forth:
Hail, for through thee the curse shall cease.
Hail, recalling of fallen Adam:
Hail, deliverance from the tears of Eve.
Hail, height hard to climb for the thoughts of men:
Hail, depth hard to scan, even for the eyes of angels.

Hail, for thou art the throne of the King:

Hail, for thou holdest Him who upholds all.

Hail, star causing the Sun to shine:

Hail, womb of the divine Incarnation.

Hail, for through thee the creation is made new:

Hail, for through thee the Creator becomes a newborn child.

Hail, Bride without bridegroom!

~

Hail, tabernacle of God the Word:

Hail, greater Holy of Holies.

Hail, ark made golden by the Spirit:

Hail, never-empty treasure-house of life.

Hail, precious crown of orthodox kings:

Hail, honored boast of godly priests.

Hail, unshaken fortress of the Church:

Hail, unconquered rampart of the Kingdom.

Hail, for through thee the standards of victory are raised on high:

Hail, for through thee our enemies are cast down.

Hail, healing of my body:

Hail, salvation of my soul.

Hail, Bride without bridegroom!

In 626 C.E., when Constantinople was besieged by the Avars, Patriarch Serge consecrated the city to the Blessed Virgin Mary. When the hostile army was dispersed and the city saved, the Akathist was chanted as a hymn of triumph and thanksgiving. It became immensely popular in the East as well as in the West and was influential in encouraging devotion to Mary. It remains the most popular devotional prayer to Mary in the Eastern Orthodox Churches. The author and origins of the prayer are unknown, but the earliest text dates from the mid-sixth century. These portions appearing here are the first and twelfth verses of this extremely lengthy hymn. Its name comes from the Greek word for standing, since tradition requires the congregation to stand while the prayer is being sung.

Salve Regina

Salve Regina, mater misericordiae, vita, dulcedo, et spes
nostra, salve.

Ad te clamamus exsules filii Hevae.

Ad te suspiramus gementes et flentes in hac lacrimarum valle.

Eia ergo, advocata nostra, illos tuos misericordes oculos ad
nos converte.

Et Jesum, benedictum fructum ventris tui, nobis post hoc
exilium ostende.

O clemens, o pia, o dulcis virgo Maria.

————

Hail holy Queen! Mother of mercy, our life, our sweetness,
and our hope!

Do thee do we cry, poor banished children of Eve;

to thee do we send up our sighs, mourning and weeping in
this valley of tears.

Turn then, O most gracious advocate, thine eyes of mercy
toward us.

And after this, our exile, show unto us the blessed fruit of thy
womb, Jesus.

O clement, O loving, O most sweet Virgin Mary.

For nine hundred years, the Salve Regina has been one of the most beloved Latin
prayers to the Virgin Mary. By tradition, it is attributed to Saint Bernard of
Clairvaux, and certainly its sentiments—although not the text—can be found in
his sermons in praise of Mary. The bulk of historical evidence indicates, however, that the most likely author of this prayer was an eleventh-century German
monk, Hermanus Contractus of Reichenau. The Salve Regina is often recited at
the conclusion of the rosary; in monasteries and convents it is sung at the end of
the day before the community retires for the night.

To the Blessed Virgin Mary

What shall I call you, full of grace?
I shall call you Heaven: for you have caused
the Sun of justice to rise.
Paradise: for in you
has bloomed the flower of immortality.
Virgin: for you have remained inviolate.
Chaste Mother: for you have carried in your arms
a Son, the God of all.
Pray to him to save our souls.

This hymn to the Blessed Virgin Mary dates from the fifth or sixth century. It is part of the Eastern Orthodox Church's Horologion, the Book of the Hours, which is the authorized collection of prayers, hymns, psalms, and sacred readings prescribed for monks and nuns. The name "Sun of justice" is one of the mystical titles for Christ.

The Kontakion of the Mother of God

Protasia ton Hristianon akateschinte, mesitia pros ton piitin ametathete, mi paridis amartolon deiseon fonas alla profthason os agathi is tin voithian imon ton pistos kravgazonton si tahinon is presvian ke spefson is ikesian, i prostatevousa ai Theotoke ton timonton Se.

————

O never-failing protection of Christians and ever-present mediation before the Creator, turn not away the prayers of us sinners, but by Thy goodness extend Thy help to us, who in faith call upon Thee: hasten, O Theotokos, to intercede for us and make speed to supplicate for us, Thou who ever protects those who honor Thee.

In the Greek Orthodox Divine Liturgy, as the priest goes in procession with the book of the Gospels, the choir sings this hymn to the Virgin Mary. The word *Theotokos* is Greek for Mother of God.

Urvasi, or Ideal Beauty

Thou art not Mother, art not Daughter, art not Bride, thou beautiful comely One,
O Dweller in Paradise, Urvasi!
When Evening descends on the pastures, drawing about her tired body her golden cloth,

Thou lightest the lamp within no home.
With hesitant wavering steps, with throbbing breast and
downcast look,
Thou dost not go smiling to any Beloved's bed
In the hushed midnight.
Thou art unveiled like the rising Dawn,
Unshrinking One!

Like some stemless flower, blooming in thyself,
When didst thou blossom, Urvasi?
That primal Spring, thou didst arise from the churning of
Ocean,
Nectar in thy right hand, venom in thy left.
The swelling mighty Sea, like a serpent tamed with spells,
Drooping his thousand towering hoods,
Fell at thy feet!
White as the kunda-blossom, a naked beauty, adored by the
King of the Gods,
Thou flawless One!

Wast thou never bud, never maiden of tender years,
O eternally youthful Urvasi?
Sitting alone, under whose dark roof
Didst thou know childhood's play, toying with gems and
pearls?
At whose side, in what chamber lit with the flashing of gems,
Lulled by the sea-waves' chant, didst thou sleep on coral bed,
A smile on thy pure face?
That moment when thou awakedst into the Universe, thou
wast framed of youth,
In full-blown beauty!

From age to age thou hast been the world's beloved,
O unsurpassed in loveliness, Urvasi!
Breaking their meditation, sages lay at thy feet the fruits of
their penance;
Smitten with thy glance, the three worlds grow restless with
youth;
The blinded winds blow thine intoxicating fragrance around;
Like the black bee, honey-drunken, the infatuated poet
wanders, with greedy heart,
Lifting chants of wild jubilation!
While thou goest, with jingling anklets and waving skirts,
Restless as lightning!

~

On the Sunrise Mount in Heaven thou art the embodied
Dawn,
O world-enchanting Urvasi!
Thy slender form is washed with the streaming tears of the
Universe;
The ruddy hue of thy feet is painted with the heart's blood of
the three worlds;
Thy tresses escaped from the braid, thou hast placed thy
light feet,
Thy lotus-feet, on the Lotus of the blossomed
Desires of the Universe!
Endless are thy masks in the mind's heaven,
O Comrade of dreams!

Hear what crying and weeping everywhere rise for thee,
O cruel, deaf Urvasi!

Say, will that Ancient Prime ever revisit this earth?—
From the shoreless, unfathomed deep wilt thou rise again,
with wet locks?—
First in the First Dawn that Form will show!
In the startled gaze of the Universe all thy limbs will be
weeping,
The waters flowing from them!
Suddenly the vast Sea, in songs never heard before,
Will thunder with its waves!

She will not return, she will not return!—that Moon of Glory
has set!
She has made her home on the Mount of Setting, has Urvasi!
Therefore on Earth today with the joyous breath of Spring
Mingles the long-drawn sigh of some eternal separation.
On the night of full moon, when the world brims with
laughter,
Memory, from somewhere far away, pipes a flute that brings
unrest,
The tears gush out!
Yet in that weeping of the spirit Hope wakes and lives,
Ah, Unfettered One!

Rabindranath Tagore (1861-1941) ranks among the most distinguished Indian humanists. He was an accomplished poet, novelist, essayist, artist, and musician. One of his most entrancing poems is this hymn to the nymph Urvasi. The Puranas tell how the nectar of immortality was lost in the ocean. To recover it, the gods troubled the waters, and from the ocean rose the beautiful Urvasi. She was immediately carried up to heaven to be the god Indra's chief dancing girl.

Salute to Fatima

Peace be upon thee, daughter of the Apostle of Allah! Peace be upon thee, daughter of the Prophet of Allah! Peace be upon thee, thou daughter of Mustafa! Peace be upon thee, thou mother of Shurafa. Peace be upon thee, thou Fifth of the People, of the Garment. Peace be upon thee, O Pure Virgin. Peace be upon thee, O daughter of the Apostle. Peace be upon thee, O spouse of our lord 'Ali al-Mustaza. Peace be upon thee, O mother of Hasan and Husayn, the two Moons, the two Lights, the two Pearls, the two Princes of the Youth of Heaven and Coolness of the Eyes of true Believers! Peace be upon thee and upon thy sire, al-Mustafa, and thy husband, our lord 'Ali! Allah honor his face and thy face and thy father's face in Paradise, and thy two sons, the Hasanayn! And the mercy of Allah and His blessings!

Islam offers prayers only to Allah. But certain individuals are so holy that they can be honored or saluted by the faithful. The English explorer and adventurer Sir Richard Burton (1821-1890), recorded that Muslim pilgrims to Medina offered this salute at the tomb of Fatima, the daughter of the Prophet Muhammad. This litany of titles honor Fatima as daughter, wife, and mother of the holiest men of Islam. She is the founder of the Shurafa, the descendants of the Prophet. The title "Fifth of the People, of the Garment" recalls a tradition that Muhammad once threw his cloak around himself, Fatima, her husband 'Ali, and their two sons Hasan and Husayn, making these five individuals one holy people, or one holy family. Hasan and Husayn, Fatima's sons, Muhammad's grandsons, are called two moons, lights, and pearls because they are double blessings, a gift from Allah given twice over. The phrase "Youth of Heaven and Coolness of the Eyes" is a metaphor for joy and gladness.

SAINT ILDEFONSUS'S PRAYER TO OUR LADY

Hail, O torrent of compassion,
river of peace and of grace,
splendor of purity, dew of the valleys:
Mother of God and mother of forgiveness.
Hail, only salvation of your children,
solemn throne of majesty,
place of shelter, temple of Christ,
the way to life, lily of chastity.
Hail, spouse of Christ,
flower of lovable grace,
humble maidservant.
Most beautiful and worthy of reverence,
no other woman was or can be like you.
We acclaim you: revered one,
your spirit is pure, and simple your heart,
chaste is your body.
You are indulgent and merciful,
dear to God, beloved above all.
The person who savors you, ardently desires you still,
still thirsts for your holy sweetness,
and always unfulfilled, confines his longing
to loving you and praising you.

In Spain, the first great theologian of the Blessed Virgin Mary was Saint Ildefonsus (617-667 C.E.), bishop of Toledo. His works are remarkable for their profound intelligence and their mysticism.

Prayer to Our Lady of Guadalupe

Our Lady of Guadalupe, mystical rose, make intercession for Holy Church, protect the Supreme Pontiff, help all those who invoke you in their necessities and since you are the Ever-Virgin Mary and Mother of the true God, obtain for us from your most holy Son the grace of keeping our faith, sweet hope in the midst of the bitterness of life, burning charity, and the precious gift of final perseverance. Amen.

Devotion to Our Lady of Guadalupe is enormously popular throughout Latin America but especially in Mexico, where she is the national patroness. Her story goes back to 1531, only ten years after Hernán Cortés conquered Mexico. An Aztec convert named Juan Diego had a vision of the Virgin Mary and reported what he saw to the bishop of Mexico City. The bishop refused to believe Juan Diego's story, so Mary caused a rose bush to bloom out of season and instructed Juan to fill his mantle with the blossoms and take them to the bishop as proof. When Juan Diego opened his cloak before the bishop, the roses cascaded to the floor. But more astonishing still was the miraculous image of the Virgin of Guadalupe that was imprinted on the robe. Today, this portrait of Mary is enshrined in a massive basilica built on the site of the apparition. The feast of Our Lady of Guadalupe is celebrated on December 12.

Hymn to Our Lady

Calm, O maiden most pure,
the wild storm of my soul,
for you alone showed yourself on earth to be
the port of all who set a course
through the perils of life.
You who gave birth to the Light,
brighten, O Pure Lady, the eyes of my heart.
You were given to us on earth
as protection, bulwark and boat.
You were given to us as a tower
and sure salvation, O maiden.
For this we no longer fear the adversary,
we who devoutly glorify you.

After many years as a monk, when he was eighty-one years old, Saint Joseph the Studite (726-832 C.E.) was appointed Metropolitan of Thessalonika. Among his writings are many hymns and homilies to the Blessed Virgin.

PRAYER AT THE TOMB OF MUHAMMAD

Assalamu 'alaika ayyuhan-Nabiyyu wa rahmatullahi wa
barakatuhu, Assalamu 'alaika ya Rasoolallah!
Assalamu 'alaika ya Nabi-Allah!
Assalamu 'alaika ya Habib Allah Assalamu 'alaika ya khaira-
khalqillah!
Assalamu 'alaika ya Shafi'-al-muznibeen!
Assalamu 'alaika wa 'ala alika wa as-habika wa ummatika
ajma'een.

———

Peace be on you, O Prophet [of God]! and His mercy and His
blessings. Peace be on you. O Messenger of God! Peace be on
you, O Prophet of God! Peace be on you, O Beloved of God!
Peace be on you, O Best in the [whole] Creation of God!
Peace be on you, O Pleader for the sinners [before God]!
Peace be on you and your descendants and your companions
and all your followers.

After Muslim pilgrims perform the required rites at Mecca, it is considered
praiseworthy for them then to go to Medina to see the tomb of the Prophet
Muhammad. There, they offer this prayer that praises Muhammad without ever
implying that he has any supernatural power to assist them. Contrary to a popular misconception in the West, the Prophet Muhammad's ascent to heaven from
Jerusalem's Temple Mount was not his final journey to the afterlife. His visit to
heaven was a special grace granted by God to give Muhammad a foretaste of the
the joys of paradise.

Michael the Victorious

Thou Michael the victorious,
I make my circuit under thy shield,
Thou Michael of the white steed,
And of the bright brilliant blades,
Conqueror of the dragon,
be thou at my back,
Thou ranger of the heavens,
Thou warrior of the King of all,
O Michael the victorious,
My pride and my guide,
O Michael the victorious,
The glory of mine eye.

I make my circuit
In the fellowship of my saint,
On the machair, on the meadow,
On the cold heathery hill;
Though I should travel ocean
And the hard globe of the world
No harm can ever befall me
'Neath the shelter of thy shield;
O Michael the victorious,
Jewel of my heart,
O Michael the victorious,
God's shepherd thou art.

Be the sacred Three of Glory
Aye at peace with me,
With my horses, with my cattle,

With my woolly sheep in flocks.
With the crops growing in the field
Or ripening in the sheaf,
On the machair, on the moor,
In cole, in heap, or stack.
Every thing on high or low,
Every furnishing and flock,
belong to the holy Triune of glory,
And to Michael the victorious.

Among the Celts, Saint Michael the Archangel was depicted riding a white horse, bearing a three-headed spear (the bright blades of the prayer) and a shield inscribed "Who is like God?" the literal translation of the archangel's Hebrew name.

Saint Michael's feast day, September 29, was a harvest festival in the Scottish islands and Highlands when the faithful went to early Mass to thank Michael for shielding their crops and herds. Then, on horseback, the entire congregation rode to the parish burial ground and made a circuit around the cemetery in honor of Michael, the angel who weighs the souls of the dead to determine if they will go to Heaven or to Hell.

The *machair* mentioned in the prayer is a Scottish term for a flat, low-lying plain. A *cole* is a stalk.

PRAYER TO SAINT MICHAEL THE ARCHANGEL

Saint Michael the Archangel, defend us in battle! Be our safeguard against the wickedness and snares of the devil. May God rebuke him, we humbly pray. And thou, O Prince of the heavenly host, by the power of God, cast into hell Satan and all the evil spirits who wander through the world seeking the ruin of souls.

Devotion to Saint Michael predates Christianity, and his role as guardian of God's people was established at least by the second century B.C.E. when the biblical Book of Daniel was written. During the persecution of the Jews under the tyrant Antiochus, the author of Daniel assured his audience that in Michael they would find a "great prince which standeth for the children of thy people" (Daniel 12:1). As early as the age of the Apostles, the Christian Church, seeing itself as the New Israel, adopted Saint Michael as its protector. In the Book of Revelations, Michael is portrayed as the captain of the angelic host that casts Satan and the other rebel angels out of heaven (Revelations 12:7-9). About the same time that Revelations was being written, in *The Shepherd of Hermas*, perhaps the earliest Christian mystical text (c. 100 C.E.), Michael is described as "the great and glorious angel Michael who has authority over this people and governs them." Although this prayer dates from much later than Revelations or *The Shepherd of Hermas*, it reflects Saint Michael's dual role as heavenly defender of Christians and their champion against the power of evil.

PRAYER TO SAINT JOSEPH IN TIME OF NEED

To you, O blessed Joseph, do we fly in our tribulation, and having implored the help of your most holy Spouse, we confidently invoke your patronage also. Through that charity which bound you to the Immaculate Virgin Mother of God, and through the paternal love with which you embraced the Child Jesus, we humbly beseech you graciously to regard the inheritance which Jesus Christ has purchased by his blood, and with your power and strength to aid us in our necessities.

O most watchful Guardian of the Holy Family, defend the chosen children of Jesus Christ; O most loving father, ward off from us every contagion of error and corrupting influence; O our most mighty protector, look with favor upon us and from heaven assist us in this our struggle with the power of darkness. And as once you rescued the Child Jesus from deadly peril, so now protect God's Holy Church from the snares of the enemy and from all adversity. Shield, too, each one of us by your constant protection so that supported by your example and your aid, we may be able to live a pious life, die a holy death, and obtain eternal happiness in Heaven. Amen.

To ensure that Christians understood that God was Christ's father, the role of Saint Joseph, husband of Mary and foster father of Jesus, was played down and even trivialized by theologians and preachers for the first fourteen hundred years of the Church's history. But by the fifteenth century, a grass-roots devotion to Saint Joseph had begun to flourish, and Pope Sixtus IV celebrated Saint Joseph's feast day in Rome in 1479. With papal recognition, Saint Joseph enjoyed a steady increase in popularity. He is invoked as defender of families, protector of virgins, and patron of fathers, workmen, the poor, the dying, and the contemplative life. In 1870, Pope Pius IX gave Saint Joseph his most exalted title, declaring him "Patron of the Universal Church." Saint Joseph's feast day is observed on March 19.

PRAYER TO ONE'S GUARDIAN ANGEL

Holy angel, to whose care this poor soul and wretched body of mine have been given, do not cast me off because I am a sinner, do not hold aloof from me because I am not clean. Do not yield your place to the Spirit of Evil; guide me by your influence on my mortal body.

Take my limp hand and bring me to the paths that lead to salvation.

Yes, holy angel, God has given you charge of my miserable little soul and body. Forgive every deed of mine that has ever offended you at any time in my life; forgive the sins I have committed today. Protect me during the coming night and keep me safe from the machinations and contrivances of the Enemy, that I may not sin and arouse God's anger.

Saint Macarius (died 390 C.E.), a monk and mystic who lived in the Scetic Desert in northern Egypt for sixty years, composed this prayer. To this day, his reputation for wisdom and eloquence is honored throughout the Eastern Orthodox Churches. The feast day of the Holy Guardian Angels is October 2.

PRAYER TO SAINT NICHOLAS

Let us come together, O feast-lovers, and praise in paeans the comeliness of Bishops, the pride of the fathers, and the fountain of miracles, the great helper of believers, saying, Rejoice, O watchman of the people of Myra, their reverend leader and unshakable pillar. Rejoice, O effulgent star, lighting the utmost corners of the world with miracles. Rejoice, O divine joy of the sorrowful, all-zealous champion of the oppressed. Wherefore, now, O all-beatified Nicholas, thou dost still intercede with Christ our God on behalf of those who ever honor faithfully and eagerly thine all-festive and joyful memory.

For at least fourteen hundred years, Saint Nicholas (died c. 348 C.E.) has remained one of the most popular saints on the calendar, both in the East and the West. He was Bishop of Myra in modern southwest Turkey, but nothing else is known about his life. The legends associated with Nicholas and the miracles attributed to his intercession are legion. He is said to have saved three impoverished women from a life of prostitution by tossing three golden balls as dowries through their bedroom window. His supernatural rescue of a storm-tossed ship made him the patron of sailors. Another legend recounts how he raised from the dead three little boys murdered by a butcher, and this tale may be the origin of Nicholas as patron of children and his evolution into Santa Claus.

This particularly effusive ode to Saint Nicholas is sung in Eastern Orthodox churches on his feast day, December 6.

HYMN TO SAINT AGNES

O happy virgin, glory but lately dawned,
O noble dweller in the celestial courts,
Adorned with thy resplendent twin diadem,
Deign now to turn thy face on our miseries.
To thee alone the Father of all has given
Power to make pure the dwelling of sin itself.
I, too, shall be made clean by thy radiant glance
If thou wilt fill my heart with its gracious light.
All is pure where thou deignest in love to dwell,
Or where thine own immaculate foot may tread.

In 304 C.E., when she was only thirteen years old, Saint Agnes was martyred in the Rome arena that stood on the site of the modern Piazza Navona. Her cult enjoyed tremendous popularity almost immediately. Saint Augustine, Saint Ambrose, and Saint Jerome all acclaimed her and encouraged devotion to her. Sometime before 349 C.E., Constantia, daughter of Constantine, the first Christian emperor, built a basilica over Agnes's tomb and a grand mausoleum for herself in the adjacent garden. Agnes is the patroness of young girls and revered as the guardian of innocence. She is always depicted with a lamb, an emblem of her own purity and a pun on her name: in Latin, the word for lamb is *agnus*.

These lines come from the conclusion of a lengthy hymn written by Aurelius Prudentius Clemens (348-c. 410 C.E.), widely considered the greatest of the early Christian Latin poets. He was born and lived in Spain, and many of his hymns celebrate the glory of the martyrs of his own country. After a pilgrimage to Rome, where he visited the shrines of the martyrs and the catacombs, Prudentius wrote his hymn to Saint Agnes.

Saint Agnes's feast day is January 21. A medieval tradition held that unmarried women who invoked Saint Agnes on the eve of her feast would see in a dream the man they would marry. This custom inspired John Keats's poem, "The Eve of Saint Agnes."

Prayer to Saint George

Deliverer of prisoners, protector of the poor, healer of the infirm and defender of kings, victorious Martyr George, pray to Christ our God for the salvation of our souls.

Saint George is one of those rare saints who enjoys a dual reputation as a heavenly patron and a cultural icon. The image of Saint George and his dragon is so well known that even people who know nothing about saints recognize it.

There is almost nothing we know with certainty about Saint George except that he was martyred, probably in Palestine, about the year 303 C.E.; he may very well have been a soldier. In the East and the West, a tremendous body of myths and legends have accumulated around George, his slaying the dragon to save a princess being the most famous. One tradition holds that George miraculously survived dozens of attempts to martyr him before dying at last on a cross. Crusaders returned home with the story of Saint George's miraculous appearance on the battlefield outside Antioch—a visitation that brought them victory. For centuries, Saint George has been considered the archetype of chivalry; he is the patron saint of England, Greece, Russia, and Catalonia. Saint George's feast day is April 23.

Prayer to Saint Spiridon

Thou hast shown thyself as a wonder-worker and a champion of the First Council, O God-inspired Father, Saint Spiridon. Wherefore thou hast conversed with a dead woman in the tomb, and thou hast converted a serpent into gold, and in the celebration of the Holy Sacraments thou wast assisted by the Angels of heaven. Glory to him who glorified thee; glory to him who crowned thee; glory to him who through thee works healing for us all.

Saint Spiridon (died c. 348 C.E.) was a shepherd and bishop of Tremithus on the island of Cyprus. He attended the Council of Nicaea—the First Council referred to in this prayer. The other references are to miraculous events from his legend. Greek Christians throughout the world honor the memory of Saint Spiridon, but he is especially venerated in Corfu, where his body is enshrined. The feast of Saint Spiridon is December 14.

PRAYER TO SAINT VLADIMIR

Thou, mighty prince Vladimir, seated upon the throne of the mother of Russian cities, the God-protected Kiev, wast like the merchant seeking goodly pearls; sending, in thy search for truth, enquirers after the Orthodox faith to Constantinople, thou hast found the pearl of great price, Christ, who chose thee as the second Paul, after whose example thou hast put off in holy Baptism all spiritual and physical blindness. Wherefore we thy people solemnly celebrate thy departure from this life. Pray for the salvation of the rulers of thy Russian kingdom.

Among Russian Christians, Saint Vladimir (c. 956-1015) is honored with the title Equal to the Apostles for the role he played in establishing Christianity in Russia. The traditional legendary account of Vladimir's conversion tells how he was inspired to send emissaries to the Jews, the Muslims, the Catholics, and the Byzantine Christians to see which religion was best. In Constantinople,

Vladimir's ambassadors were dazzled by the churches and the rituals, so much so that they could not tell if they were in heaven or on earth. Based on these reports, Vladimir brought Russia into the fold of the Eastern Rite.

It is a wonderful story, but most likely Vladimir converted after his marriage to the Byzantine princess Anne, daughter of Emperor Basil II, as another way to seal his alliance with his imperial neighbor.

Vladimir was an enthusiastic convert, founding many churches and monasteries and urging—often compelling—his subjects to accept Christianity. His feast day is celebrated on July 15.

PRAYER IN HONOR OF THE HOLY CROSS

We adore the tree of thy Cross, O Lover of mankind; for thou wast nailed thereon, O life of all, and didst open paradise, thou Savior of the thief, who, having confessed thee, became worthy of bliss, crying, Remember me, O Lord. Receive us, therefore, as thou receivest him, as we cry to thee, We have all sinned. By thy compassion, turn not away from us.

At Matins on the Feast of the Elevation of the Cross (September 14), this prayer is chanted in Eastern Orthodox churches. The thief alluded to in the prayer is the Good Thief, by tradition named Dismas, who was crucified with Jesus. As he hung on his cross, Dismas repented and acknowledged Christ as the Son of God. Jesus promised him, "Today shalt thou be with me in paradise" (Luke 23:40-43).

Blessings on the Earth and Its People

To Earth the Mother of All

I will sing of well-founded Earth, mother of all, eldest of all beings. She feeds all creatures that are in the world, all that go upon the goodly land, and all that are in the paths of the seas, and all that fly: all these are fed of her store. Through you, O queen, men are blessed in their children and blessed in their harvests, and to you it belongs to give means of life to mortal men and to take it away. Happy is the man whom you delight to honor! He has all things abundantly: his fruitful land is laden with corn, his pastures are covered with cattle, and his house is filled with good things. Such men rule orderly in their cities of fair women: great riches and wealth follow them: their sons exult with ever-fresh delight, and their daughters in flower-laden bands play and skip merrily over the soft flowers of the field. Thus is it with those of whom you honor, O holy goddess, bountiful spirit.

Hail, Mother of the gods, wife of starry Heaven; freely bestow upon me for this my song substance that cheers the heart!

Earth, also known as Gaia, was also invoked as the Universal Mother and eventually became identified with the goddesses Demeter and Cybele. This hymn, which acclaims Earth as the source of all power, fertility, and prosperity, would have been sung in one of her temples. As with all the Homeric hymns, authorship is uncertain, but the hymns date between the eighth and the sixth centuries B.C.E.

Thanksgiving for the Beauty of the World at Harvest Time

Father in Heaven, we thank thee for all this world of thy providence, so fertile in wonders, so rich in beauty to every hungering sense of man. We thank thee for thy loving-kindness and thy tender mercy, while thou with equal care watchest over the sparrow's fall, and holdest all worlds in thy arms of never-ending love. We thank thee for the beauty which thou bringest forth in every stream of water, on every hillside, and that wherewith thou fringest the paths of men as they pass to their daily work. We bless thee for the beauty which thou gatherest in the lily's fragrant cup, clothing it with a kinglier loveliness than Solomon in all his glory ever could put on. But we thank Thee still more that in a tenderer and lovelier and holier way thou revealest thy loving-kindness, and thy tenderness, and thy holiness to thy children. Thou hast endowed us with senses to receive the world of sight and sound, and to be fed and beautified therewith. Thou hast given us spiritual powers which lay hold of justice, and truth, and love, and faith in thee. Thou hast fed our souls with thyself. Lord, what shall we render thee for the least of these thy mercies? We pray thee that we may live as blameless as the flowers of the field; that our lives within may be as fragrant and without as fair, and that what is promise in our spring, what is blossom in our summer, may, in the harvest of heaven, bear fruit of everlasting life; through Jesus Christ our Lord. Amen.

This Anglican prayer that celebrates the beauty of the natural world and the abundant gifts God gives his people alludes to Christ's Sermon on the Mount, found in Saint Matthew's gospel. "Consider the lilies of the field, how they grow; they toil not, neither do they spin: And yet I say unto you, that even Solomon in all his glory was not arrayed like one of these" (Matthew 6:28-29).

THE PLOUGHING VEDA

Lord of the field, pour for us,
like the cow pouring milk, a sweet stream
that drops honey and is pure as holy butter.
May the Lords of the Law shower on us grace.

Sweet be the herbs to us and waters,
and for us the mid-air be full of sweetness.
Let the Lord of the field be sweet to us,
and may we follow him uninjured.

May the draught-bulls work happily,
and happily our men,
and happily the plough furrow.
May the traces happily bind.
Wield the goad happily.

Suna and Sira, be pleased with this our hymn,
and, with the milk you have made in heaven
besprinkle this earth.

Rig-Veda IV, 57

Suna represents the ploughshare. Sira represents the plough. In this ancient Hindu hymn, these essential tools are personified as divine spirits and invoked to bless the planting season.

AKHENATEN'S GREAT HYMN TO ATEN

You shine out in beauty on the horizon of heaven, O living
Aten, the beginning of life.
When you have appeared on the eastern horizon, you have
filled every land with your perfection.
You are beautiful and great, bright and high above every land;
your rays encompass the lands to the very limit of all you
have made. You are Re and reach to their limit and restrain
them for your beloved son [Akhenaten].

Although you are far away, your rays are on earth;
although you are in man's countenance, no one knows your
going. When you set on the western horizon, the earth
lies in darkness as in death.

The sleepers are in their rooms, their heads veiled, and no
eye beholds another.
All that they have under their heads may be stolen—but they
do not notice.
Every lion has come forth from its den, and all the snakes bite.
The earth lies in silence, [for] the one who created it has
gone to rest on his horizon.

The earth becomes bright: you have arisen on the horizon.
As Aten you shine by day and have driven away the darkness.
You shed your rays, and the two lands are in festive mood.
The men of the sun are awakened and stand upon their feet;
you have raised them up.
They wash their bodies and take their clothing, their arms
are bent in worship, because you appear.

The whole land goes to work.

All beasts are satisfied with their pasture, the trees and plants become green.

The birds flutter in their nests, raising their wings in worship before your spirit.

All the lambs skip around, the birds and everything that flutters live because you have risen for them.

The ships sail upstream and down, every way is open because you appear.

The fish in the river dart before your face, for your rays penetrate into the depths of the sea.

You make the seed grow in women, make fluid into mankind; you keep the child alive in its mother's womb and soothe it so that it does not weep, you are the nurse even in the mother's womb.

You are the one who gives breath to all that he has made, to preserve life.

When he descends from the womb to breathe on the day of his birth, you open his mouth completely to speak and supply his needs.

When the chick in the egg already speaks in the shell, you give him breath within to keep him alive.

You have given him strength to break it [the egg].

He comes forth from the egg to speak with all his power, and walks on his legs as soon as he emerges.

How manifold are your works!

They are hidden from the face [of man], O sole God, apart from whom there is no other!

You have made the earth according to your desire, while you were alone,

with men, cattle and all beasts, everything that is on earth
going on its feet,
everything that is on high flying with its wings,
the foreign lands of Syria and Nubia and the land of Egypt.
You set every man in his place and see to his needs;
each one has his food and his time of life is reckoned;
their tongues are separate in speech, and their nature is
likewise; the color of their skin is different:
you distinguish the peoples.

You create the Nile in the underworld and bring it up at your
pleasure,
to sustain the people of Egypt as you have made them,
the Lord of all of them, wearying himself with them,
the Lord of the whole land, rising for them,
Aten of the day, great in majesty.

All the distant hill countries, you also make them so that
they can live,
for you have set a Nile in heaven, and it comes down for them;
it makes waves on the mountains like a sea, to water their
fields by their settlements.
How generous are your plans, Lord of eternity!
The Nile in heaven is there for the foreign peoples and for all
the wild beasts of the desert which go on their feet.
But the [true] Nile comes from the underworld of Egypt.

Your rays make all plants grow tall:
when you rise, they live and grow for you.
You created the seasons, in order to make all your creation
thrive: the winter to cool them, the heat that they may
taste you.

You made the sky distant in order to rise in it and to see all
that you have made,
while you were alone, rising in your changeable forms as the
living Aten, appearing, shining, far and yet near.

You make millions of forms from yourself, the one, cities and
towns, fields, roads and the river.
Every eye beholds you over against them, for you are the
Aten of the day, high over the earth.
There is no other who knows you, but your son
Nefer-kheperu-Re Wa-en-Re [Akhenaten],
for you have made him to know your plans and your
strength.

The world is in your hands, as you have made it.
When you have risen, they live,
and when you set, they die,
for you are a lifetime yourself;
men live in you.
Eyes look on perfection until you set.
All work is laid aside when you set on the right hand.
When you rise again, you make every arm stir for the king, and
haste is in every limb, since you have founded the earth.
You raise them [creatures] for your son who came forth from
your body,
the king of Upper and Lower Egypt, who lives from order,
Akhenaten, and the great royal consort, Nefertiti.

During his reign (1365-1348 B.C.E.), the pharaoh Akhenaten forbade the
Egyptians to worship any god but Aten, the sun. This hymn, an original work by
Akhenaten, was inscribed in hieroglyphs on the tomb of Ay in Tell el-Amarna.
The parallels between this hymn and Psalm 104, which follows, are striking.

Bless the Lord, O my soul.

O Lord my God, thou art very great; thou art clothed with honor and majesty.

Who coverest thyself with light as with a garment: who stretchest out the heavens like a curtain:

Who layeth the beams of his chambers in the waters: who maketh the clouds his chariot: who walketh upon the wings of the wind:

Who maketh his angels spirits; his ministers a flaming fire:

Who laid the foundations of the earth, that it should not be removed for ever.

Thou coveredst it with the deep as with a garment: the waters stood above the mountains.

At thy rebuke they fled; at the voice of thy thunder they hasted away.

They go up by the mountains; they go down by the valleys unto the place which thou hast founded for them.

Thou hast set a bound that they may not pass over; that they turn not again to cover the earth.

He sendeth the springs into the valleys, which run among the hills.

They give drink to every beast of the field: the wild asses quench their thirst,

By them shall the fowls of the heaven have their habitation, which sing among the branches.

He watereth the hills from his chambers: the earth is satisfied with the fruit of thy works.

He causeth the grass to grow for the cattle, and herb for the

service of man: that he may bring forth food out of the earth;
And wine that maketh glad the heart of man, and oil to make his
face to shine, and bread which strengtheneth man's heart.
The trees of the Lord are full of sap; the cedars of Lebanon,
which he hath planted;
Where the birds make their nests: as for the stork, the fir
trees are her house.
The high hills are a refuge for the wild goats; and the rocks
for the conies.
He appointeth the moon for seasons: the sun knoweth his
going down.
Thou makest darkness, and it is night: wherein all the beasts
of the forest do creep forth.
The young lions roar after their prey, and seek their meat
from God.
The sun ariseth, they gather themselves together, and lay
them down in their dens.
Man goeth forth unto his work and to his labor until the evening.
O Lord, how manifold are thy works!
In wisdom hast thou made them all: the earth is full of thy
riches.
So is this great and wide sea, wherein are things creeping
innumerable, both small and great beasts.
There go the ships; there is that leviathan, whom thou hast
made to play therein.
These wait all upon thee; that thou mayest give them their
meat in due season.
That thou givest them they gather: thou openest thine hand,
they are filled with good.
Thou hidest thy face, they are troubled: thou takest away
their breath, they die, and return to the dust.
Thou sendest forth thy spirit, they are created: and thou

renewest the face of the earth.

The glory of the Lord shall endure for ever: the Lord shall rejoice in his works.

He looketh on the earth, and it trembleth: he toucheth the hills, and they smoke.

I will sing unto the Lord as long as I live: I will sing praise to my God while I have my being.

My meditation of him shall be sweet: I will be glad in the Lord.

Let the sinners be consumed out of the earth, and let the wicked be no more.

Bless thou the Lord, O my soul.

Praise ye the Lord.

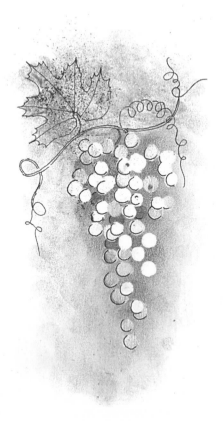

MYSTICAL POEM OF RUMI (23)

Bring into motion your amber-scattering trees; bring into dancing the souls of the Sufis.

Sun, moon and stars dancing around the circle, we dancing in the midst—set that midst a-dancing.

Your grace minstrelwise with the smallest melody brings into the wheel the Sufi of heaven.

The breeze of spring comes hurrying, uttering a melody; it sets the world a-laughing, raises autumn from the dead.

Many a snake becomes a friend, rose partners thorn; the season of scattering largesse is come to the king of the orchard.

Every moment a perfume wafts from the garden like a message come whither, as if to say, "Cry welcome today to the friends!"

The orchard, departed into its secret heart, is speaking to you; do you depart into your own secret, that life may come to your soul,

That the lily's bud may open its secret to the cypress, that the tulip may bring good tidings to willow and judas-tree,

That the secret of every young shoot may emerge from the depths, the ascensionists having set up a ladder in the garden.

The songbirds and nightingales are seated in the branches, like the guardian enjoying his stipend from the treasury;

These leaves are like tongues, these fruits like hearts—when the hearts show their faces, they give worth to the tongue.

There is a tradition that says that while Saint Francis of Assisi was in Egypt and the Holy Land in 1219, he encountered the mystical poems of Rumi and that these works influenced Francis's own great Canticle of the Sun.

Saint Francis of Assisi's Canticle of the Sun

In the Original Italian

Altissimu, omnipotente, bonsignore,
tue sono le laude, la gloria et l'honore
et omne benedictione.

Ad te solo, Altissimo, se Confano
et nullu homo enne dignu
te mentovare.

Laudato sie, mi signore, cum tucte le tue creature,
spetialmente messer lo frate sole,
loquale iorni et allumini noi per lui.

Et ellu e bellu eradiante cum grande splendore:
de te, Altissimo, porta significatione.

Laudato si, mi signore, per sora luna ele stelle:
in Celu lai formate clarite
et pretiose et belle.

Laudato si, mi signore, per frate vento,
et per aere et nubilo et sereno et omne tempo
per loquale a le tue creature dai sustentamento.

Laudato si, mi signore, per sor aqua,
laquale e multo utile et humile
et pretiosa et casta.

Laudato si, mi signore, per frate focu,
per loquale ennalumini la nocte:

et ellu ebello et iocundo
et robustoso et forte.

Laudato si, mi signore, per sora nostra matre terra,
laquale ne sustenta et governa,
et produce diverse fructi
con coloriti flori et herba.

Laudato si, mi signore, per quelli ke perdonano
per lo tuo amore
et sostengo infirmitate
et tribulatione.

Beate quelli kel susterranno in pace,
ca da te, Altissimo,
sirano incoronati.

Laudato si, mi signore, per sora nostra
morte corporale,
da laquale nullu homo
vivente po skappare.

Guai acqueli ke morrano
ne le peccata mortali!

Beati quelli ke trovarane
le tue santissime voluntati,
ka la morte secunda
nol fara' male.

Laudate et benedicite, mi signore,
et rengratiate et servite lo
cum grande humilitate.

O most high, potent, sweet Lord,
To you belong the praise, the glory, the honor and all blessing.

To you alone, Most High, they look for life,
And no man may fitly speak your Name.

With all your creatures, Lord, be praised,
Not least for our Brother Sun, who daily brings us light.

Beautiful and radiant in his great splendor
How well he tells of thee, Most High.

Be praised, my Lord, for Sister Moon and stars,
Carved by you, clear and rich and fair.

Be praised, my Lord, for Brother Wind,
For air in every mood and time through whom you give your
creatures sustenance.

Be praised, my Lord, for Sister Water,
So useful, humble, precious and chaste.

Be praised, my Lord, for Brother Fire,
Which lightens us by night, fine and merry and healthy and
strong.

Be praised, my Lord, for our Sister, Mother Earth,
Who holds us up and keeps us straight, yielding diverse fruits
and flowers of different hue, and grass.

Be praised, my Lord, for those who find forgiveness
in their hearts for your love's sake,
And bear with sorrow and affliction.

Blessed they who bear these in peace
Because by you, Most High, they will be crowned.

Praised be my Lord for our Sister mortal death,
From whom no man alive will escape.

Woe to those who die in mortal sin!

Blessed are those who are found walking in your
most holy ways
For the second death will bring them no evil.

O praise and bless my Lord,
Thanking him and serving him with great humility.

Saint Francis of Assisi (1182-1226) composed his Canticle of the Sun in 1225. He wrote it in his native Italian—not Latin—imitating the poetic style of the troubadours. Francis seems to have added to the Canticle from time to time and it may have had many more verses that were forgotten or perhaps never heard personally by Brother Leo, one of the saint's closest friends and the first person to write down the Canticle. We know that Francis added the verses on forgiveness when arbitrating a dispute between the governor and the bishop of Assisi, and he composed the verses to Sister Death as he lay on his deathbed, October 2 and 3, 1226.

Hymn to the Sun

Hail to thee, thou sun of the seasons,
As thou traversest the skies aloft;
Thy steps are strong on the wing of the heavens,
Thou art the glorious mother of the stars.

Thou liest down in the destructive ocean
Without impairment and without fear;
Thou risest up on the peaceful wave-crest
Like a queenly maiden in bloom.

During his travels in the late nineteenth and early twentieth centuries, Alexander Carmichael observed that it was a custom among men in the Scottish islands to uncover their heads when they saw the sun rise and sing this hymn under their breath.

To the Sun

Up rises the beautiful orb
on the near margin of the sky,
as the divine white-colored steed bears it fast
making it visible to all.

The Sun, shining on all, crest by crest,
the lord of what moves and what stands still,
the seven sister bays bear in the chariot
for the well-being of the world.

That eye, divinely placed, rising bright,
may we see for a hundred autumns.
And may we live for a hundred autumns.

Rig-Veda VII, 66, 14-16

This Vedic hymn describing the Sun as being drawn across the heavens in a chariot will remind readers of the Greek god Helios, who drove his sun chariot across the sky. The "seven sister bays" refer to seven mares who represent the rays of the sun.

Good Wishes

Power of raven be thine,
Power of eagle be thine,
Power of the Fiann.

Power of storm be thine,
Power of moon be thine,
Power of sun.

Power of sea be thine,
Power of land be thine,
Power of heaven.

Goodness of sea be thine,
Goodness of earth be thine,
Goodness of heaven.

Each day be joyous to thee,
No day be grievous to thee,
Honor and compassion.

Love of each face be thine,
Death on pillow be thine,
Thy Savior's presence.

The strong pre-Christian element that makes up the greater part of this blessing suggests its antiquity. Alexander Carmichael recorded it in South Uist in the Outer Hebrides.

Lighting the Sabbath Candles

Baruch atah Adonai elohaynu melech ha'olam asher kidshanu be'mitzvotav vetzivanu l'hadlik ner shel Shabbat.

———

Blessed art Thou O Lord our God, King of the Universe, who has made us holy with thy commandments and instructed us to light Sabbath candles.

The Jewish Sabbath begins at sundown on Friday when women light two (or more) Sabbath candles. If there are no women in the house, then the law mandates that a man must light two Sabbath candles. In some households, it is a tradition to light additional candles—one for each child in the family.

Once the candles are lit, the father blesses each of his children. Over the heads of the boys he says, "May God make you like Ephraim and Menashe," the two sons of the patriarch Joseph. And over the girls he says, "May God make you like Sarah, Rebecca, Rachel, and Leah," the wives of Abraham, Isaac, and Jacob.

The Havdalah Blessings

Baruch ata, Adonai Eloheinu, melech haolam, borei peri hagafen.
Baruch ata, Adonai Eloheinu, melech haolam, borei minei vesamim.
Baruch ata, Adonai Eloheinu, melech haolam, borei meorei haeish.

Baruch ata, Adonai Eloheinu, melech haolam, hamavdil bein kodesh lechol, bein or lechoshech, bein yom hashevi'i lesheishet yemei hama'aseh.

Baruch ata, Adonai, hamavdil bein kodesh lechol.

———

Blessed art Thou, O Lord our God, King of the universe, who createst fruit of the vine.

Blessed art Thou, O Lord our God, King of the universe, who createst various kinds of spices.

Blessed art Thou, O Lord our God, King of the universe, who createst the lights of fires.

Blessed art Thou, O Lord our God, King of the universe, who hast made a distinction between the sacred and the profane, between light and darkness, between the seventh day and the six working days. Blessed art Thou, O Lord, who hast made a distinction between the sacred and the profane.

Havdalah means "separation" because these blessings, recited on Saturday night, mark the end of the Jewish Sabbath and the return to the workday world. By tradition, as the wine is blessed, it is poured to overflow the cup as a sign of both generosity and prosperity. The fragrant spices are to help worshipers recall the sweetness of the Sabbath until it returns again next week. And the flame that lights the havdalah candle symbolizes the end of the day of rest—lighting a fire and performing all types of labor (all of which are forbidden during the Sabbath) are once again permitted.

BLESSING A BONFIRE

O Lord God, Father almighty, unfailing Ray and Source of all light, sanctify (*make the Sign of the Cross*) this new fire, and grant that after the darkness of this life we may come unsullied to thee Who art Light eternal. Through Christ our Lord. Amen.

Before the coming of Christianity, most peoples in ancient Europe lit bonfires at the summer solstice. When Europe became Christian, the Roman Catholic Church "baptized" the custom of the bonfire by creating a blessing for the blaze and encouraging the celebration of the solstice on June 23, the eve of the Feast of Saint John the Baptist. This blessing comes from *The Roman Ritual*, a comprehensive collection of blessings authorized by the Roman Catholic Church for public or private use.

LIGHTING THE HANUKKAH LIGHTS

Baruch ata, Adonai Eloheinu, melech haolam, asher kideshanu
bemitsvotav, vetsivanu lehadlik neir shel Chanuka.
Baruch ata, Adonai Eloheinu, melech haolam, sheasa nisim
la'avoteinu bayamim haheim lazeman hazeh.
Baruch ata, Adonai Eloheinu, melech haolam, shehecheyanu
vekiyemanu vehigianu lazeman hazeh.

————

Blessed art Thou, O Lord our God, King of the universe, who
hast sanctified us with thy commandments, and commanded
us to light Hanukkah lights.
Blessed art Thou, O Lord our God, King of the universe, who
didst perform miracles for our fathers in those days, at this
season.
Blessed art Thou, O Lord our God, King of the universe, who
hast granted us life and sustenance and permitted us to reach
this season.

Hanukkah commemorates the victory in 167 B.C.E. of the Maccabees over the Syrian tyrant Antiochus, who had outlawed the practice of Judaism and defiled the Temple in Jerusalem. To reconsecrate the Temple, pure olive oil had to burn without ceasing in the sanctuary, but the Maccabees could find only enough to burn for a single day. Miraculously, this small amount of oil continued to burn for eight days, until more consecrated oil could be brought to replenish the lamp.

To celebrate this miracle, Jews light candles every night during the eight-day festival of Hanukkah. As the candles are lit, the first two blessings given above are recited. The third blessing is said only on the first night of the festival.

A Prayer to Hestia to Bless a Home

Hestia, in the high dwellings of all, both deathless gods and men who walk on earth, you have gained an everlasting abode and highest honor: glorious is your portion and your right. For without you mortals hold no banquet, where one does not duly pour sweet wine in offering to Hestia both first and last.

And you, Slayer of Argus, Son of Zeus and Maia, messenger of the blessed gods, bearer of the golden rod, giver of good, be favorable and help us, you and Hestia, the worshipful and dear. Come and dwell in this glorious house in friendship together; for you two, well knowing the noble actions of men, aid on their wisdom and their strength.

Hail, Daughter of Cronos, and you also, Hermes, bearer of the golden rod! Now I will remember you and another song also.

As goddess of the hearth, Hestia was worshipped in every household throughout ancient Greece. This hymn would have been sung to her at the blessing of a home or in her temples. It is thought to date between the eighth and sixth centuries B.C.E.

Prayer at the Foundation of a House

Let us pray to the Lord. Lord have mercy.

O God Almighty, Who made the Heavens with wisdom and has established the earth upon its sure foundations, the Creator and Author of all men, look upon these Your servants [Names], to whom it has seemed good to set up a house for their dwelling in the dominion of Your Power, and to rear it by building; establish it upon a stable rock, and found it according to Your divine word in the Gospel, so that neither wind, nor flood, nor any other thing shall be able to harm it; graciously grant that they may bring it to completion, and deliver all them who shall wish to dwell therein from every attack of the enemy; for Yours is the dominion, and Yours is the Kingdom, and the Power, and the Glory, of the Father, and of the Son, and of the Holy Spirit, both now and ever, and to the ages of ages. Amen.

Standing at a building site, an Eastern Orthodox priest pronounces this blessing. By alluding to the parable of the man who built his house on rock (Luke 6:47-49), the priest asks God both to make the inhabitants' home secure and to strengthen their faith.

PRAYER WHEN ONE IS TO TAKE UP ABODE IN A NEW HOUSE

Let us pray to the Lord. Lord have mercy.

O God our Savior, Who did deign to enter under the roof of Zaccheus, unto salvation of the same and of all that were in the house; do you, the same Lord, keep safe also from harm them who now desire to dwell here, and who, together with us unworthy ones, do offer unto You prayer and supplication:

Bless this (*the priest makes the Sign of the Cross*) their home and dwelling, and preserve their life free from all adversity; for unto You are due all glory, honor and worship, as also unto your Eternal Father, and Your All-Holy, Good and Life-creating Spirit; both now and ever, and unto ages of ages. Amen.

This Eastern Orthodox blessing refers to Zaccheus, a tax collector at Jericho and a man despised by his neighbors as a public sinner. Since he was of small stature, Zaccheus climbed into a sycamore tree so he could see Jesus. Jesus saw Zaccheus in the tree and asked him to come down. "I mean to stay in your house today," he said. Zaccheus hurried down, welcomed Christ as an honored guest, and repented his sins. The story is found in Luke 19:1-10.

BLESSING OF A HOME

Peace be unto this home.

And unto all who dwell herein.

Sprinkle me with hyssop, O Lord, and I shall be clean: wash me, and I shall be whiter than snow.

Be merciful to me, O God, for great is thy goodness. Glory be to the Father, and to the Son, and to the Holy Spirit. As it was in the beginning, is now, and ever shall be,

world without end. Amen.

O Lord, hear my prayer.

And let my cry come unto thee.

The Lord be with you.

And with your spirit.

Let us pray. Hear us, holy Lord, almighty Father, eternal

God! And deign to send thy holy angel from heaven to guard,

cherish, protect, visit, and defend all who dwell in this home.

Through Christ our Lord. Amen.

In Roman Catholic theology, God consecrates all of creation—not just humankind. It is fitting, then, that every good thing, or anything that leads to a good result, should also be blessed and consecrated. Blessings in the Catholic faith are sacramentals, or extensions of the seven sacraments. The Sacrament of Matrimony, for example, is extended by the blessing of the home, the expectant mother, the mother after childbirth, and the many objects that are used in the life of the family. These blessings may be thought of as the allies of the great seven sacraments, bringing God's presence into even the humblest dimension of life.

BLESSING OF A MOTHER AFTER CHILDBIRTH

Our help is in the name of the Lord.

Who made heaven and earth.

This woman shall receive a blessing from the Lord and

mercy from God, her Savior, for she is of the people

who seek the Lord.

Enter the temple of God, adore the Son of the Blessed Virgin

Mary, Who hath given thee fruitfulness of offspring.

Lord, have mercy on us. Christ, have mercy on us. Lord, have mercy on us.

Our Father, who art in heaven, hallowed be thy name. Thy kingdom come, thy will be done on earth as it is in heaven. Give us this day our daily bread, and forgive us our trespasses as we forgive those who trespass against us. And lead us not into temptation, but deliver us from evil.

Preserve thy handmaid, O Lord.

Who trusts in thee, my God.

Send her, Lord, aid from on high.

And from Sion watch over her.

Let the enemy have no power over her.

And the son of evil do nothing to harm her.

O Lord, her my prayer.

And let my cry come unto thee.

The Lord be with you.

And with your spirit.

Let us pray. Almighty, everlasting God, Who through the delivery of the Blessed Virgin Mary has turned into joy the pains of the faithful at childbirth, look kindly upon this thy handmaid who comes rejoicing into thy holy temple to make her thanksgiving. Grant that after this life she together with her offspring may merit the joys of everlasting bliss, by the merits and intercession of the same Blessed Mary.

May the peace and blessing of almighty God, Father, Son, and Holy Spirit come upon thee, and remain for all time. Amen.

This special blessing for mothers who have recently given birth is one of the most ancient rites of the Church. This form comes from *The Roman Ritual*.

A Father Blesses His Son

Father:	Son:
Akongo [God] of the ancestors,	mokanga
Akongo of the fathers,	mokanga
Our Akongo.	mokanga
When you go	mokanga
You must walk on the right path	mokanga
And return in strength,	mokanga
Return bearing your spear,	mokanga
Return wearing your war-belt,	mokanga
And light of foot,	mokanga
Bless, Kunda, bless!	

Before a Ngombe leaves home, his father recites this blessing over him, while the son responds "mokanga," the equivalent of "Yes" or even "Amen." Kunda, who is invoked at the end of the blessing, is believed to be the founder of many of Zaire's Ngombe clans.

A Blessing for Families

Almighty God, our heavenly Father, who settest the solitary in families; We commend to thy continual care the homes in which thy people dwell. Put far off from them, we beseech thee, every root of bitterness, the desire of vainglory and the pride of life. Fill them with faith and virtue, knowledge, temperance, patience, godliness. Knit together in constant affection those who, in holy wedlock, have been made one flesh; turn the heart of the fathers to the children, and the heart of the children to the fathers; and so kindle charity among us all that we be evermore kindly affectioned with brotherly love; through Jesus Christ our Lord. Amen.

For ten years, Episcopal clergy in the United States assembled prayers, blessings, and services that had developed in Episcopal congregations. These special offices, as they are called, were then collected in a small volume and published in 1929. The prayers found in *The Offices for Special Occasions* are in the tradition of the *Book of Common Prayer*, and in many cases even imitate the cadences of that great sixteenth-century prayer book.

GRACE BEFORE MEALS

May he who gave a feast of dew and drink from a rock,
Who turned flowing water into Falernian wine,
And who walked dry-shod upon the waves,
In his kindness bless his gifts to his servants.

This prayer is found in a manuscript of eighth- and ninth-century texts and is said to have been inscribed on the refectory wall of an unknown monastery in France during the reign of Charlemagne.

BLESSING BEFORE MEALS

The eyes of all hope in thee, O Lord, and thou wilt
give them food in due time. Thou openest thy hand,
and fillest every living thing with thy blessing.

This grace is often recited in Roman Catholic monasteries, convents, and other
religious communities.

BLESSING OF BREAD

Our help is in the name of the Lord.
Who made heaven and earth.
The Lord be with you.
And with your spirit.
Let us pray. O Lord, Jesus Christ, bread of angels,
living bread unto eternal life, bless this bread as thou
didst bless the five loaves in the wilderness; that all
who eat it with reverence may through it attain the
corporal and spiritual health they desire. Who livest
and reignest eternally. Amen.

This Roman Catholic blessing recalls the five loaves of bread by which Christ
miraculously fed five thousand people in the wilderness, and the Sacred Host—
"bread of angels"—by which Christ nourishes the souls of the faithful.

Grace after Meals

Leader:

Gentlemen, let us say grace.

Company, then Leader:

Blessed be the name of the Lord henceforth and forever.

Leader:

With your consent, let us now bless (our) God whose food we have eaten.

Company, then Leader:

Blessed be (our) God whose food we have eaten and through whose goodness we live.

All:

Blessed be he and blessed be his name.

Blessed art thou, Lord our God, King of the universe, who sustainest the whole world with goodness, kindness and mercy. Thou givest food to all creatures, for thy mercy endures forever. Through thy abundant goodness we have never yet been in want; may we never be in want of sustenance for thy great name's sake. Thou, O God, sustainest all, doest good to all, and providest food for all the creatures thou hast created. Blessed art thou, O Lord, who dost sustain all.

We thank thee, Lord our God, for having given a lovely and spacious land to our fathers as a heritage; for having taken us out of slavery; for thy covenant which thou hast sealed in our flesh; for thy Torah which thou hast taught us; for thy laws which thou hast made known to us; for the life, grace and kindness thou hast bestowed on us; and for the sustenance thou grantest us constantly, daily, at every season, at every hour.

When three or more Jewish men have eaten a meal together, this blessing is recited. The words in parentheses are added if a *minyan*—ten adult Jewish men—is present. For the Sabbath and certain festivals, the grace is expanded to include additional prayers.

BLESSING OF YOUNG CROPS AND VINEYARDS

Our help is in the name of the Lord.
Who made heaven and earth.
The Lord be with you.
And with your spirit.
Let us pray. We appeal to thy graciousness, O almighty God, that thou wouldst shower thy blessing upon these first-fruits of creation, which thou hast nurtured with favorable weather, and mayest bring them to a fine harvest. Grant also to thy people a sense of constant gratitude for thy gifts, so that the hungry may find rich nourishment in the fruits of the earth, and the needy and the poor may praise thy wondrous name. Through Christ our Lord. Amen.

Virtually every religious tradition in every time and place has a spring blessing for fields, crops, and vineyards. This blessing comes from the Roman Catholic book, *The Blessings*.

BERAKHOT:
JEWISH BLESSINGS RECITED ON VARIOUS OCCASIONS

Over bread:

Baruch atah Adonai elohaynu melech ha'olam hamotzi lechem min ha'aretz.

——

Blessed art thou, Lord our God, King of the Universe, who bringest forth bread from the earth.

Over wine:

Baruch atah Adonai elohaynu melech ha'olam boray pri ha'gafen.

——

Blessed art thou, Lord our God, King of the Universe, who createst the fruit of the vine.

On seeing a rainbow:

Baruch atah Adonai elohaynu melech ha'olam zocher ha'berit ve'ne'eman bivrito vekayam be'ma'amaro.

——

Blessed art thou, Lord our God, King of the Universe, who rememberest thy covenant and keepest thy promise faithfully.

On seeing trees blossoming:

Baruch atah Adonai elohaynu melech ha'olam shelo chisar

b'olamo davar uvara vo briyot tovot v'ilanot tovim l'hanot bahem b'nai adam.

———

Blessed art thou, Lord our God, King of the Universe, who hast withheld nothing from thy world; and hast created therein beautiful creatures and goodly trees for the enjoyment of mankind.

On seeing a person of abnormal appearance:
Baruch atah Adonai elohaynu melech ha'olam mishaneh ha'briyot.

———

Blessed art thou, Lord our God, King of the Universe, who dost vary the aspect of thy creatures.

On seeing a person of profound Torah wisdom:
Baruch atah Adonai elohaynu melech ha'olam shechalak me'chochmato lirey'av.

———

Blessed art thou, Lord our God, King of the Universe, who hast imparted of thy wisdom to those who revere thee.

On seeing a person of profound secular learning:
Baruch atah Adonai elohaynu melech ha'olam she'natan me-chochmato l'vasar va'dam.

———

Blessed art thou, Lord our God, King of the Universe, who hast imparted of thy wisdom to flesh and blood.

On hearing bad tidings:

Baruch atah Adonai elohaynu melech ha'olam dayan ha-emet.

———

Blessed art thou, Lord our God, King of the Universe, the true Judge.

On hearing good tidings:

Baruch atah Adonai elohaynu melech ha'olam hatov v'hametiv.

———

Blessed art thou, Lord our God, King of the Universe, who art good and beneficent.

By ancient tradition, every Jewish blessing begins with the formula, "Blessed art thou, Lord our God, King of the Universe" before it addresses the particular person or things to be blessed. Many of the blessings selected here date back over twenty-three hundred years and are attributed to Jewish sages known collectively as the Men of the Great Assembly. In the Middle Ages, Moses Maimonides distinguished three types of blessings: blessings that one recites before eating, drinking, or smelling something pleasant; blessings recited before one fulfills a commandment of the Lord or performs a good deed; and blessings that give praise and thanks to God for his wonderful works or which ask God for his assistance. In every instance, the blessings remind the faithful that the works of humankind pale before the wonders God performs and the mysteries he reveals every day.

THE BLESSING OF THROATS

Through the intercession of Saint Blaise, bishop and martyr, may God preserve you from every evil of the throat and from all other evils. In the name of the Father, and of the Son, and of the Holy Spirit.

Saint Blaise was martyred in Sebaste in what is now Turkey about the year 316 C.E. According to legend, he saved a child who had a fish bone caught in his throat by making a cross with two candles and blessing the boy. On Blaise's feast day (February 3), Catholic priests place two crossed candles at the throat of each member of the congregation and recite this blessing.

BLESSING AN ICON

O Lord our God, Who created us after Your own Image and Likeness; Who redeems us from our former corruption of the ancient curse through Your man-befriending Christ, Who took upon himself the form of a servant and became man; Who having taken upon Himself our likeness remade Your Saints of the first dispensation, and through Whom also we are refashioned in the Image of Your pure blessedness.

Your Saints we venerate as being in Your Image and Likeness, and we adore and glorify You as our Creator; wherefore we pray You, send forth Your blessing upon this icon, and with the sprinkling of hallowed water, bless and make holy this icon unto Your glory, in honor and remembrance of Your Saint [Name].

And grant that this sanctification will be to all who venerate this icon of Saint [Name], and send up their prayer unto You standing before it.

Through the grace and bounties and love of Your Only-Begotten Son, with Whom You are blessed together with Your All-Holy, Good and Life-creating Spirit; both now and ever, and unto ages of ages. Amen.

In the Orthodox Church, an icon is blessed so it can be installed in a church, home, or any other suitable place. In return, the icon sanctifies the place where it is set up; it is for the faithful a tangible reminder of the Divine Presence. According to Orthodox theology, to pray before an icon is to pray in the presence of Christ, or of the Mother of God, or of the saint depicted. The icon is the point where heaven and earth meet.

TORAH BLESSINGS

Barechu es Adonai hamevorach.

Baruch Adonai hamevorach leolam vaed.

Baruch ata, Adonai Eloheinu, melech haolam, asher bachar banu mikol ha'amim, venasan lanu es Toraso.

Baruch ata, Adonai, nosein hatorah.

———

Bless the Lord who is blessed.

Bless the Lord who is blessed forever and ever.

Blessed art Thou, O Lord our God, King of the universe, who hast chosen us from all peoples, and hast given us thy Torah.

Blessed art Thou, O Lord, Giver of the Torah.

Before the reading of the Torah—the sacred scroll that contains the first five books of the Bible—the above blessings are recited by the reader and the congregation. Jewish law permits the Torah to be read whenever a *minyan* of ten adult Jewish males are present. In some congregations, ten adults, male or female, comprise a *minyan*.

BLESSING OF A SCHOOL

Hear us, O holy Lord, Father almighty, eternal God, and send thy holy angel from heaven to guard, cherish, protect, visit, and defend all who assemble, teach, and study in this building. Through Christ our Lord. Amen.

Blessing of Schoolchildren

Watch over our school, O Lord, as its years increase, and bless and guide her children wherever they may be, keeping them ever unspotted from the world. Let their hearts be warm with the flame of their childhood's ideals, their faith unshaken, their principles immovable. Be thou by their side when the dark hour shall come upon them; strengthen them when they stand, comfort and help them when they are weak-hearted, raise them up if they fall. Let the cross never grow dim to their eyes, but through the struggles and sufferings that may attend their steps, let its radiance lead them heavenward, and in their hearts may thy peace which passeth understanding abide all the days of their life; through Jesus Christ our Lord. Amen.

Blessing of a Library

O God, Who art the Lord of all learning, pour forth thy blessing (*make the Sign of the Cross*) upon this library. Let it safely withstand fire and every peril, and permit it to increase its volumes from day to day. May all who come here as officials or students make progress in knowledge of things human and divine, and increase likewise their love for thee. Through Christ our Lord. Amen.

The three school-related blessings given above were all composed in the twentieth century. The first and third come from the Catholic book, *The Blessings*; the third is from the Episcopalian *The Offices of Special Occasions*.

Blessing of a Boat

Graciously hearken to our prayers, O Lord, and with thy holy hand bless (*make the Sign of the Cross*) this boat and all who sail hereon, as thou didst deign to bless Noah's Ark in its course during the Deluge. Stretch forth to them, O Lord, thy right hand, as thou didst reach out to Peter when he walked upon the sea. Send thy holy angel from heaven to guard this boat and ever keep it safe from every peril, together with all on board. And when threatened dangers have been removed, comfort thy servants with a calm voyage and the desired harbor. And having successfully transacted their business, recall them again when the time comes to the happiness of country and home. Thou Who livest and reignest forevermore. Amen.

This Catholic blessing contains two seafaring allusions to the Bible. The first recalls the story of the Ark in which Noah and his family and a pair of every type of creature were all saved from the Deluge. The second story appears in Saint Matthew's Gospel (Matthew 14:30-31). Once, when Peter and some of the other apostles were out fishing, they saw Christ coming toward them, walking on the water. Peter, ever zealous, leapt out of the boat to meet Jesus. When he began to sink, Christ grasped Peter's hand and brought him to safety.

Blessing of Any Vehicle of Travel

May Christ our true God, through the intercession of His all-pure Mother, through the protection of the bodiless powers, of the holy, glorious and all-praiseworthy Apostles, and of Saint Nicholas, and all the Saints, have mercy on us and save us, as he is good and loves mankind.

The "bodiless powers" referred to in this Orthodox Christian blessing are the angels, who are pure spirit. Saint Nicholas in the Eastern Churches is venerated as the patron of travelers.

The Priestly Blessing (Dukhaning)

Y'varech'cha Adonai v'yishm'recha
Yaeir Adonai panav eilecha vichuneka
Yisa Adonai panav eilecha v'yaseim l'cha shalom.

———

May the Lord bless thee and keep thee.
May the Lord make his face to shine upon thee and be gracious unto thee.
May the Lord lift up his countenance upon thee, and give thee peace.

Numbers 6:24-26

Aaron, the brother of Moses, was the first priest, and his descendants today enjoy the special privilege of blessing Jewish congregations. At a certain point of the synagogue service, the *Kohanim*, or priests, remove their shoes, stand before the community, raise their hands, and recite this blessing. In the Orthodox tradition, it is customary for men to cover their faces with their prayer shawls during the blessing since it is believed that God's presence is manifest where the priests are standing.

PONTIFICAL BLESSING

Sit nomine Domini benedictum.

Ex hoc nunc et usque in saeculum.

Adjutorium nostrum in nomine Domini.

Qui fecit coelum et terram.

Benedicat vos omnipotens Deus: Pater, et Filius, et Spiritus Sanctus. Amen.

———

May the name of the Lord be blessed.

Both now and forever.

Our help is in the name of the Lord.

Who made heaven and earth.

May Almighty God bless you: (*make the Sign of the Cross*)

the Father, and the Son, and the Holy Spirit.

In the Roman Catholic faith, any bishop may give his congregation this solemn Pontifical Blessing. Nonetheless, it is a blessing that is most commonly associated with the Pope. It concludes every Mass that the Holy Father celebrates, and it is the blessing that he imparts to the assembly at the end of an audience.

INDEX BY RELIGIOUS TRADITION

Hindu

Islam

Jewish

Index of First Lines

Eternal rest grant unto them, O Lord *162*

Father in Heaven! Show unto us a little patience *186*
Father in Heaven, we thank thee for all this world *256*
Father, have pity on me *25*
For wisdom is more active than all active things *133*

Gentlemen, let us say grace *285*
Give me Thy grace, good Lord *182*
Give us grace, O God, to dare *176*
Gloried and sanctified be God's great name *161*
God is Greater! *13*
God tests as gold *101*
Graciously hearken to our prayers, O Lord *294*

Hail, you Former *31*
Hail holy Queen *232*
Hail Mary, full of grace *10*
Hail to the Amida Buddha *21*
Hail to the Name of Shiva *17*
Hail to the worshipful Lord Vishnu *17*
Hail to thee, thou new moon *51*
Hail to thee, thou sun of the seasons *270*
Hail, for through thee joy shall shine forth *230*
Hail, O Lord, Great Power, Great Might *109*
Hail, O torrent of compassion *239*
Harei at mekudeshet *144*
Have done with pride and arrogance *102*
Have mercy upon me, O God *87*
He is God; what he does is right *158*
He is the eternal Lord who reigned *28*
Hear us, O holy Lord *292*
Hear, O Israel *3*
Heavenly Father, make us, we pray thee *39*
Hestia, in the high dwellings *277*
Holy angel, to whose care *247*
Holy, holy, holy is the Lord of Hosts *112*
Holy, holy, holy, Lord God of hosts *113*

Holy, Most High, terrible *106*
Homage to Thee, Perfect Wisdom *132*
Homage to the Lotus Sutra *21*
Homage, Rudra, to thy wrath and thy arrow *191*

I arise today *188*
I arouse Indra, the Merchant *207*
I bathe thy palms *144*
I begin in the name of God *99*
I begin to sing about Poseidon *177*
I believe in God, the Father almighty *4*
I confess to Almighty God *83*
I create not just one negative action in a day *89*
I lie down tonight *42*
I mean to be obedient *94*
I render my thanks to thee, everlasting King *38*
I take refuge in the Great Awakening *223*
I trample on thee, thou seizure *173*
I will sing of well-founded Earth *255*
In paradisum *162*
In the beginning was God *5*
In the beginning was the Divinity in his splendor *19*
In the beginning was the Word *6*
In the market, in the cloister—only God I saw *62*
In the Name of God, the Beneficent, the Merciful *14*
Ineffable Creator, who from the treasures of your wisdom *181*

Kadosh, Kadosh, Kadosh *112*
Kol nidre weesare waharame *95*

La ilaha ill-Allah, Muhammad-ur-rasool ullah *12*
La ilaha ill-Allahu *12*
Last night I saw Poverty in a dream *76*
Late have I loved you, O Beauty, so ancient and so new *70*
Let every devout and God-loving man *54*
Let justice seize old Adam's crew *104*
Let the whole of mankind tremble *108*
Let us come together, O feast-lovers *248*

Let us fall down before the majesty of our God *90*
Let us, who mystically represent the Cherubim *107*
Libera nos, quaesumus, Domine *221*
Live you two here, be not parted *148*
Lo! I am the slave of Allah *105*
Lord Jesus Christ, Son of the living God *11*
Lord of the field, pour for us *257*
Lord of the springtime *41*
Lord, as we gather here in the middle of the night *45*
Lord, our master: she of the jade skirt *23*
Lord, you have taken the fear of death away *150*
Love divine, all loves excelling *64*

Magnificat anima mea Dominum *118*
Make haste, O Christ our God *187*
Man, that is born of a woman *154*
May Christ our true God *295*
May he who gave a feast of dew *283*
May it be thy will, Lord our God *178*
May the angels lead you to Paradise *162*
May the Lord bless thee and keep thee *295*
May the name of the Lord be blessed *296*
May there be voice in my mouth *171*
May you be for us a moon of joy and happiness *50*
Most sweet Jesus, may your sacred body and blood *68*
My eternal Lord and Father *193*
My heart is capable of every form *16*
My heart is dying though it lives *62*
My heart is wounded, O Master *61*
My Lord! Make this a region of security *205*
My soul doth magnify the Lord *118*

Namu Amida Butsu *21*
Namu myo ho renge kyo *21*
Now must we praise the Guardian *117*
Nu sculon herigean *117*
Nyankonpon Tweaduapon Nyame *143*

O blessed poverty 75
O Earth, wherever it be my people dig 203
O God Almighty, Who made the Heavens with wisdom 278
O God our Savior, Who did deign to enter 279
O God! Pardon our living and our dead 167
O God! verily do I seek refuge in Thee 84
O God, do not put out this lighted lamp 174
O God, with each day that passes I grow more deficient 80
O God, from whom proceed all holy desires 219
O God, give us a heart 174
O God, I have neither a key to open a door 80
O God, our help in time of need 222
O God, Who art the Lord of all learning 293
O good and innocent dead 168
O happy virgin, glory but lately dawned 249
O Holy God 10
O immeasurably tender love! 73
O Lord and Master of my life 79
O Lord God, Father almighty, unfailing Ray and Source 275
O Lord God, we humbly beseech thee to direct our thoughts 37
O Lord Jesus Christ, bread of angels 284
O Lord Jesus Christ, who Thyself didst weep beside the grave 157
O Lord our God, Who created us after Your own image 290
O Lord, punish me not in thy anger 176
O Lord, we are not worthy to have a glimpse of heaven 100
O Lord, you who have measured the heights 85
O merciful God, grant that as Christ died and rose again 141
O most high, potent, sweet Lord 268
O most sweet and loving Lord 65
O my father Osiris 155
O my God, I am heartily sorry 83
O my God, the best of Thy gifts 74
O my Lord, the stars are shining 40
O never-failing protection of Christians 234
O quick! defend me from the claws of the dog 196
O sun, as you arise in the east 37
O ye Compassionate Ones 165
Of many mouths and eyes 124

St. Michael the Archangel, defend us in battle *245*
Subhanak-Allahumma wa bihamdika *15*
Subvenite sancti Dei *162*
Supreme Sky God who alone is great *143*

Te Deum laudamus *129*
Teach me, O God, not to torture myself *186*
The Beneficent . . . *120*
The cattle, my! *201*
The edges of the years have met *53*
The eyes of all hope in thee, O Lord *284*
The Father has chosen us out of grace *66*
The Gazelles. I say the Gazelles *142*
The little drop of the Father *140*
The Lord is my shepherd *33*
The lord of beauty and quintessence of loveliness *72*
The maidens that go yonder *172*
The peace in the sky, the peace in the mid-air *218*
The successful, victorious, skillfully gaming Apsara *208*
The warrior of the sacred bundle now starts *213*
The whole world is coming *25*
There is no god but God *12*
There is no King but him whom I have seen *93*
There is none like our God *27*
There is none worthy of worship but God *12*
There, where the darts are dyed *214*
This am I, that are thou *146*
This woman shall receive a blessing from the Lord *280*
Thou art consecrated unto me *144*
Thou art not Mother, art not Daughter *234*
Thou hast shown thyself as a wonder-worker *250*
Thou Michael the victorious *243*
Thou who didst pray for them that crucified thee *226*
Thou, mighty prince Vladimir *251*
Thou, O Tsui-goab! *52*
Through the intercession of Saint Blaise *290*
'Tis the gift to be simple *26*
To you, O blessed Joseph, do we fly in our tribulation *246*

Up rises the beautiful orb *271*

Veneration to the Blessed One *22*

Watch over our school, O Lord *293*
Watch over thy child, O Lord *141*
We abuse, we betray, we are cruel *81*
We adore the tree of thy Cross *252*
We appeal to thy graciousness, O almighty God *286*
We are poured on the enemy like a mighty torrent *212*
We praise thee, O God *130*
What earthly pleasure remains unmixed with grief *166*
What shall I call you, full of grace *233*
When the foot in the night *195*
Who is an enemy to Gabriel *230*
Who is there who has not sinned against his god *85*
With the souls of the righteous dead, give rest *166*

Y'varech'cha Adonai v'yishm'recha *295*
Yisgaddal v'yiskaddash *160*
You are the guardian of the bounds of revelation *110*
You shine out in beauty on the horizon *258*
You Thunderers are our eldest brothers *204*
You who bridle colts untamed *126*
You, Father God, Who are in the heavens and below *175*
You, my forefathers, you have congregated here *151*

PERMISSIONS

"A Prayer of Saint Augustine" from *Augustine of Hippo: Selected Writings*, translated and with an introduction by Mary T. Clark (New York: Paulist Press, 1984). Reprinted by permission of Paulist Press.

"Ti-sarana-gamana (Taking the Three Refuges)" from *Buddhism*, edited by Richard A. Gard (New York: George Braziller, Inc., 1962).

"Sleep Consecration," "Good Wishes," "Blessing of Brigit," "Michael the Victorious," "Unction Prayer," "Charm for Seizure," "Hymn to the Sun," "The Invocation of the Graces," "Birth Baptism," and "To the New Moon" from Alexander Carmichael, *Carmina Gadelica: Hymns and Incantations Collected in the Highlands and Islands of Scotland in the Last Century* (Hudson, New York: Lindisfarne Books, 1992). Reprinted by permission of Lindisfarne Books, Hudson, New York 12534.

"A Prayer of Saint Catherine of Siena" from *Catherine of Siena: The Dialogue*, translated and with an introduction by Suzanne Noffke, O.P. (New York: Paulist Press, 1980). Reprinted by permission of Paulist Press.

"Ein Keilo-heinu (There Is None Like Our God)," "Torah Blessings," "Berakhot: Jewish Blessings Recited on Various Occasions," "Grace After Meals," "The Priestly Blessing (Dukhaning)," "Lighting the Hanukkah Lights," "The Havdalah Blessings," "Mourners' Kaddish," "Prayer for the Sick," "Prayer for Rain," "For a Safe Journey," "Night Prayer," and "Adon Olam (Master of Eternity)" from *Daily Prayer Book: Ha-Siddur Ha-Shalem*, translated, annotated and with an introduction by Philip Birnbaum (New York: Hebrew Publishing Company, 1977).

"Prayer of Saint Thomas Aquinas Before Study" from *Devoutly I Adore Thee: The Hymns and Prayers of Saint Thomas Aquinas*, edited and translated by Robert Anderson and Johann Moser (Manchester, New Hampshire: Sophia Institute Press, 1993). Copyright © 1993 by Robert Anderson and Johann Moser. Reprinted by permission of Sophia Institute Press, Box 5284, Manchester, New Hampshire 03108.

"Confession to Tara," "The Praises of Padma Sambhava," and "The Meditation of Chenresig" from *The Diamond Light: An Introduction to Tibetan Buddhist Meditations*, compiled by Janice Dean Willis (New York: Simon & Schuster, 1972).

"The Father Has Chosen Us out of Grace," "God Tests As Gold," and "My Eternal Lord and Father" from *Early Anabaptist Spirituality: Selected Writings*, translated by Daniel Liechty (New York: Paulist Press, 1994). Reprinted by permission of Paulist Press.

"Prayer to One's Guardian Angel," "Prayer of Saint Macrina on Her Deathbed," "Hymn to Christ the Savior," "A Woman's Prayer," "The Prayer of Saint Genesius of Rome," and "Prayer for Use on Saturdays" from *Early Christian Prayers*, edited by A. Hamman, OFM, translated by Walter Mitchell (London: Longmans, Green & Co., Ltd., 1961). Reprinted by permission of Addison Wesley Longman Ltd.

"The First Principle of Islam," "The Obligatory Prayers of Islam," "Declaration of the Oneness of God (The Creed of Islam)," "The Refutation of Disbelief (Kalimatu raddil-kufr)," "The Tawaf," "The Call to Prayer (Azan)," "Islamic Funeral Prayers," and "Prayer at the Tomb of Muhammad" from Muhammad Abdul Aleem Siddiqui, *Elementary Teachings of Islam* (Chicago: Kazi Publications, 1985). Reprinted by permission of Kazi Publications.

"Hymn to Saint Agnes" from *Fathers of the Church*, vol. 43: *The Poems of Prudentius*, translated by Sister M. Clement Eagan CCVI (Washington: The Catholic University of America Press, 1962). Reprinted by permission of The Catholic University of America Press.

"Canticle of the Sun" from Michael de la Bedoyere, *Francis: A Biography of the Saint of Assisi* (New York: Image Books/Doubleday, 1962).

"A Prayer of Saint Francis of Assisi," "A Prayer of Saint Clare of Assisi," and "Saint Clare of Assisi's Canticle to Poverty" from *Francis and Clare: The Complete Works*, translated and with an introduction by Regis J. Armstrong, OFM Cap, and Ignatius C. Brady, OFM (New York: Paulist Press, 1982). Reprinted by permission of Paulist Press.

"Tantra of Tara," "From the Hindu Marriage Rite," "Krishna Manifests Himself in His Glory," "The Living Dead," "A Prayer for Success in Gambling," "Praise of Rama As the Supreme Being," "Charm to Stop the Flow of Blood," "Yearning and Love for God," "Urvasi, or Ideal Beauty," and "Death at Hand" from *Hinduism*, edited by Louis Renou (New York: George Braziller Inc., 1962).

"A Prayer of Thomas à Kempis" from Thomas à Kempis, *The Imitation of Christ*, translated by William C. Creasy (Notre Dame: Ave Maria Press, 1989). Copyright © 1989 by Ave Maria Press, Notre Dame, Indiana 46556. Reprinted by permission of the publisher.

"To the Blessed Virgin Mary," "Saint Ildefonsus's Prayer to Our Lady," "Hymn to Our Lady" from *In Praise of Mary: Hymns from the First Millenium of the Eastern and Western Churches* (Middlegreen, England: St. Paul Publications, 1981).

"The Bris Milah," "Naming a Newborn Daughter," and "A Mother's Prayer at a Bris Milah" from Nathan Gottlieb, *A Jewish Child Is Born* (New York: Bloch Publishing Company, 1960).

"The Akathist Hymn to Our Lady" from *The Lenten Triodion*, translated by Mother Mary and Archimandrite Kallistos Ware (London/Boston: Faber & Faber, 1978). Reprinted by permission of Faber & Faber Ltd.

"A Prayer of Saint Teresa of Avila" from *Lingering with My Lord: the Post-Communion Experiences of Saint Teresa of Avila*, introduction and translation by Michael D. Griffin, O.C.D. (New York: Alba House, 1984). Reprinted by permission of Alba House.

"The Manifestation of Mithras" from *The Mithras Liturgy*, edited and translated by Marvin W. Meyer (Missoula, Montana: Scholars Press, 1976). Reprinted by permission of Scholars Press.

Prayers 4, 19, 52, and 72 from Khwajih 'Abd Allah Ansari, *Munajat: The Intimate Prayers*, translated by Lawrence Morris and Rustam Sarfeh, M.D. (New York: Khaneghah and Maktab of Maleknia Naseralishah, 1975). Reprinted by permission of Khaneghah and Maktab of Maleknia Naseralishah.

"Universal Tolerance" from Annemarie Schimmel, *The Mystical Dimensions of Islam* (Chapel Hill: The University of North Carolina Press, 1975). Copyright © 1975 by The University of North Carolina Press. Reprinted by permission of the publisher.

Poems 23, 41, and 394 from Jala al-Din Rumi, *Mystical Poems of Rumi 1: First Selection of Poems 1-200*, translated by A. J. Arberry (Chicago: The University of Chicago Press, 1968). Reprinted by permission of The University of Chicago Press.

"Hymn to the Creator," "Aztec War Song," and "Prayer to the Supreme Dual God" from *Native Mesoamerican Spirituality: Ancient Myths, Discourses, Stories, Doctrines, Hymns, Poems from the Aztec, Yucatec, Quiche-Maya and Other Sacred Traditions*, edited by Miguel Leon-Portilla (Ramsey, New Jersey: Paulist Press, 1980). Reprinted by permission of Paulist Press.

"An Akkadian Invocation to an Unnamed God," and "Akhenaten's Great Hymn to Aten" from *Near Eastern Religious Texts Relating to the Old Testament*, edited by Walter Beyerlin, translated by John Bowden (Philadelphia: The Westminster Press, 1978). Reprinted by permission of Westminster John Knox Press.

"A Litany of the Beautiful Names of Allah" from *The Ninety-Nine Names of Allah*, edited by Ira Friedlander (San Francisco: Harper San Francisco, 1993). Copyright © 1978 by Shems Friedlander. Reprinted by permission of HarperCollins Publishers, Inc.

"Petitions from the Sacrament of Marriage," "Blessing of Any Vehicle of Travel," "Blessing an Icon," "Prayer in Time of Trouble," "Prayer at the Foundation of a House," and "Prayer When One Is to Take Up Abode in a New House" from *An Orthodox Prayer Book*, translated by Father John von Holzhausen and Father Michael Gelsinger (Brookline, Massachusetts: Holy Cross Orthodox Press, 1977). Reprinted by permission of Holy Cross Orthodox Press.

"In the Beginning Was God," "For a Day Full of Blessings," "Prayer at the New Moon," "Prayer at the 'Yearly Killing' Festival," "For Life to My People," "Litany for the Initiation Ceremony," "At the First Menstruation Ceremony," "To Welcome Raided Cattle into the Fenced Homestead," "To the Earth, Forest and Rivers at the Sowing Season," "Protection against

Snake Bite," "At a War Ritual around the Sacred Rock," "For Help in Sickness," "Let Us Weep Softly," "Prayer to the Living Dead Who Once Shared This Life," and "A Father Blesses His Son" from John S. Mbiti, *The Prayers of the African Religion* (Maryknoll, New York: Orbis Books, 1975). Copyright © 1975 by John S. Mbiti. Reprinted by permission of the author.

Two prayers of Søren Kierkegaard from *The Prayers of Kierkegaard*, edited by Perry D. LeFevre (Chicago: The University of Chicago Press, 1956). Reprinted by permission of The University of Chicago Press.

"Two Prayers at Midnight" from *Praying with the Orthodox Tradition*, compiled by Stefano Parenti (Crestwood, New York: St. Vladimir's Seminary Press, 1996). Reprinted by permission of St. Vladimir's Seminary Press.

"Rabi'a's Evening Prayer," "A Vision of God," "Rabi'a's Prayer for Mystical Union," and "Salute to Fatima" from Margaret Smith, *Rabi'a* (Fountain Valley, California: One World Publishing, 1994).

"The Invocation of the Buddhas and Bodhisattvas" from *The Tibetan Book of the Dead*, edited by W. Y. Evans-Wentz (Oxford: Oxford University Press, 1956). Reprinted by permission of Oxford University Press.

"A Prayer Before Holy Communion," "A Prayer of Saint Sarrah," and "Saint Ephraim's Prayer at Midnight" from *Voices in the Wilderness: An Anthology of Patristic Prayers*, edited and translated by Nikolaos S. Hatzinikolaou (Brookline, Massachusetts: Holy Cross Orthodox Press, 1988). Reprinted by permission of Holy Cross Orthodox Press.

RD10DD